EDUCATION UNBOUND

How to Create Educational Opportunity

in Abundance

James Pitt and Ken Webster

Education Unbound
How to Create Educational Opportunity in Abundance
© 2021 James Pitt and Ken Webster

First Edition published in 2021 by TerraPreta
Enquiries to publishing@terra-preta.co.uk
ISBN 978-0-9559831-1-5

Price £17.90
Print on Demand by IngramSpark, 2021
Every effort has been made to ensure that URLs are correct at time of going to press. If any copyright holders have been overlooked the publisher will be pleased to include any necessary credits in subsequent reprints and additions.

Front cover and illustrations: Oliver Pitt
Back cover, page layout and prepress: Debs Oakes

Acknowledgements

This book is extracted from a longer work called *What's next? Education as though learners matter.* James and Ken wish to thank the many friends and family members who inspired, read and critiqued various drafts, especially Jonathan, Ben, Laurie, Oliver and Sophie Pitt, Dorrie Brown, Catherine Heinemeyer, Michael Woosnam-Mills and Sara Heinrich. Tamasin Greenough Graham made a huge contribution to the extensive research which underpinned the whole project. We also are most grateful to Oliver Pitt for the cover design and illustrations, and Debs Oakes for design and layout and help in getting it to press.

Dedication

This book is dedicated to teachers everywhere and especially those who struggle to make the most of a failing system. In particular it is dedicated to the memory of Denny Lane, and Socrates. May the ideas expressed be a support and challenge to all those who seek a better way.

WHAT OTHERS HAVE SAID

"This book reminds us that learning is an effect of the communities we belong to, whether those are schools, friendship groups, families, clubs or digital networks. It also suggests that learning is a transformational process at personal, social and political levels. The book is timely as well as deeply engaging."

Richard Andrews, Professor in Education, University of Edinburgh

"This is a much-needed clarion call for education once again to be about the full development of an individual, including all their creativity, curiosity, sense of adventure and fun and enquiry, not just about the absorption of received wisdom. It is important and significant."

Lord Chris Smith, Master of Pembroke College, Cambridge

"Learning is central to who we are as humans. Learning excites us, motivates and fulfils us. The opportunity for learning exists all around us, in every person that we meet, and throughout our lives. What we experience in schools should be the starting point for a lifetime of curiosity, learning and excitement - and this is what the schooling system should be evaluated on, the ability for people to go into the world and deploy creativity and energy in every aspect of their lives. This book focuses attention on what needs to change in formal educa-

tion; but this needs to be matched with the creation of opportunities and infrastructures for continual, informal learning, peer-to-peer, in our neighbourhoods and cities."

Tessy Britton, Founding Chief Executive and Head of Design, Participatory City Foundation

"A good educator doesn't teach - they share their view, engendering a love of learning and creative curiosity that becomes life's foundation. As the world has changed, it's time education caught up. In this important book James Pitt and Ken Webster have shared their view, and it is inspiring."

Susan Scurlock MBE, Founder and CEO Primary Engineer

"Abundance, participation, passion and a hope for humanity are themes that ring through this book which offers a well-balanced view of opportunities and possibilities for an education system with a strong moral purpose. Creating school communities which enable and inspire the 'turning over of a stone to see what lies beneath' and the 'unfolding of a person' seems to me to be a place where learning will lead to success. If we can co-create a curriculum that allows for spontaneity, stretching beyond zones of comfort and a habitual examination of assumptions, we are more likely to bring about sustainable change and better futures for all."

Victoria Pendry, CEO The Curriculum Foundation.

"I worked with both James Pitt and Ken Webster over many years. It comes as no surprise to me that they have produced this short book which challenges the status quo in education. It provides a manifesto for those who wish to be informed and take action to improve the educational opportunities for all young people so that they are empowered to meet the challenges facing the world."

Dr. David Barlex, formerly Director of the Nuffield Design & Technology Project

"Politicians, media types and university admissions tutors are complicit with millions of parents around the world in re-enforcing the morass that is state education. Its raison d'être remains success in exams. This book is a manifesto for freedom whose message demands serious study by everyone with a stake in the education of our children; Pitt and Webster evoke a new and enlightened future for them. A wonderful, practical and engaging guide to reform."

Phil Andrews, Entrepreneur, Investor and CEO of Get Field Ready

"The current one-size-fits-all approach to learning and assessment brings much unnecessary stress and anxiety to young people. It creates a competitive environment, where the joy of learning is stifled and where individuality and difference are mocked, rather than being mutually celebrated. This timely book offers hope,

not just for education, but for the world's health and happiness."

Fran Guilding, Family Counsellor

"I've taught students of different ages for 20 years, I've seen bright, enthusiastic students devastated by poor exam results with an increasing number suffering from anxiety which undermines their enthusiasm and natural love of learning. James Pitt and Ken Webster argue convincingly for far more project–based learning, with learners encouraged to follow their interests and take greater responsibility. The community learning exchanges suggest an innovative way forward ... where do I sign up?"

Carol Sheward, secondary school teacher of Design Technology

"I wish my teachers had read this book ...."

Sam Brown, Joiner

"A timely exploration of how an education policy centred on easily measurable testing has deprived a whole generation of children of a love of learning, and the freedom and security that brings. This is a necessary and important call for radical change."

Angela Warren, Teacher and Education Adviser

CONTENTS

Part Three: A way forward – returning education to the learners

Foreword by Sir Anthony Seldon

This is a brave book. It will be dismissed by conventional thinkers and the status quo as another crazy outpouring from La La Central. I suspect that the authors would be entirely happy with them thinking that.

To appreciate this book, one has to have a mind far more open than that possessed by the great majority so caught up in the education world in the UK and internationally that they have lost the ability to stand back and see clearly. One has indeed to be brave and independent to ask the most basic of questions: what is education for? Why do we have schools? Why do we tolerate a system that fails so many students, teachers, parents and society? For all the undoubted good that the current system does, could it in fact be doing far better?

I am a total product of the establishment. I attended an elite public boarding school, an elite university, and for 20 years, I ran elite public schools before spending five years running Britain's first independent university, founded by Margaret Thatcher no less.

To be honest, I don't know why and how I acquired the thoughts that I have about education after an experience like that. It has been mostly in the independent sector. But that is because, on many occasions, my attempts to move over to the state sector were rebuffed. Who knows how I might have changed the state sector had I been allowed into it. Perhaps not at all: but I was not given the chance, so I had to try to change it from the outside.

This brief book points to many extraordinary thinkers, including Leo Tolstoy, John Dewey and more recently, Ken Robinson. It discusses ground-breaking movements like the French L'École Mutuelle, the international Steiner-Waldorf schools, Italy's Reggio Emilia schools and the frustrating but still magnificent International Baccalaureate, which for 50 years has set the pace globally on curriculum and assessment.

Readers do not have to agree with all of what follows in this book – I find parts of it challenging myself – to find it extraordinarily liberating and thoughtful. Its brevity is a real strength. It can be read in little over an hour, but it will help change you and those who you encounter for a lifetime.

Anthony Seldon

Sir Anthony Seldon is one of the best-known educators in Britain, and the only person alive to have run schools and a university. He was Head of Brighton College and Wellington College, before becoming Vice-Chancellor of the University of Buckingham. He founded the Festival of Education, the Festival of Higher Education, and inspired The Times' national education commission. He is a leader in many education fields including well-being and AI. He is also author or editor of 50 books on British PMs, contemporary history, politics and education, was the first director of the Institute for Contemporary British History, is co-founder of Action for Happiness, and is honorary historical adviser to 10 Downing Street.

INTRODUCTION

*T*his is a book about hope, and the place of education in forging a new and more caring humanity.

Our present education system does not offer a way out of pandemics, climate change, populist demagoguery and inequality. It serves to reinforce all of these as it is built on the propagation of a 'me first' culture. By turning learning into a commodity, the education system sells the false promise that working hard and passing exams is a route to self-actualisation and happiness.

It isn't. Most people leave formal education into a world of debt, the increasing casualisation of labour and the shift to a rentier economy. Fewer people own a greater proportion of the nation's assets and most people find it harder to access the things they need in life – healthy food, affordable housing, meaningful occupation and conviviality. And real education.

What might happen if we redesign education as a social project through which the many have an opportunity to develop their own potential rather than do what someone else decides is good for them and be examined on it? What might happen if we return learning to the learners rather than fragment and package it into discrete bundles? Can we reconnect learning to the communities in which people live, and at the same time explore the limitless possibilities of an interconnected world? Can we have more fun and find joy in our learning, becoming more playful and happier in the process? And in doing so develop agency and resilience among the many?

We believe we can. We are at a critical moment in the history of humanity when the social and economic forces that held each other in tension and gave the appearance of stability have shifted. They are no longer in balance and life will have to change.

This short book is about these issues. Part One looks at some liberating approaches to learning. Part Two examines the larger forces at play in the world today. Part Three proposes a way forward.

It is absolutely not an attack on teachers. Virtually no one in the education professions designed or even asked for this knowledge-loaded system. Vast numbers of them are crying out for change. We do not pit skills and creativity as alternatives to knowledge. Knowledge is vital in all walks of life. However, deep, lasting, meaningful knowledge comes when a learner has a thirst for it.

The book is part of a manifesto for a future which values democracy over coercion, in which organisation is participatory and power is distributed. It is a route to bring back fun and meaning after the pandemic has moved on.

PART ONE: LEARNER-CENTRED EDUCATION

HOW TO CREATE EDUCATIONAL OPPORTUNITY IN ABUNDANCE

"Children are missing out on their education." "We have to get children back into school as quickly as possible." "It's not fair because the children can't go to school so they're not going to be educated." "How can they catch up on what they have missed?"

Such cries from the media, from politicians, from parents and indeed teachers miss the point as to what education is. What they are talking about is schooling. This book is about seizing the opportunities opened by the pandemic to plan a parallel system of education, one which will genuinely prepare for future uncertainties.

The pandemic has shown that schools have a huge role in society. In many places they act as a community hub. They are a safe space which otherwise children might not have at home or in the community. They are place where children can get a square meal. These are all really important functions in society, and we need them to be fulfilled, but they are not the same as education. In this book we are proposing a new vision of education that opens up new possibilities for society.

A child being educated at home might miss these benefits but profit from other things like going outside, turning over a stone and seeing what's living underneath it. They might have more opportunities to ride a bike, enjoy internet gaming, participate in sport or write a story. With less school the child might have more time to pursue their own interests and take things to a deeper level than they'd be able to do otherwise. The child might have other children and adults around with whom they are able to talk about whatever interests them. Covid-19 has created terrible conditions for many people, and larger economic changes (which we address in Part Two) mean that many people will not go back to the work they did. The potential plus side is vast numbers of adults in every community with knowledge and skills they might share. This is an exciting opportunity.

The pandemic is causing huge disruptions. In 2020, exams were cancelled in the United Kingdom and again in 2021. Will the world survive without exams? Exams are often seen as the be-all and end-all of educational endeavour. Yet they do not measure education.

This book is about education in the UK and in particular England and Wales. But the systemic problems that we describe are true in all countries where governments have imposed a statutory curriculum and prescribed assessment regimes. Equally, the creative possibilities of education for freedom are applicable anywhere. This is why we have dedicated the book to teachers everywhere and especially those who are trying to hollow out niches in which their learners can thrive, even if the system is stacked against them.

The UK education system operates as a production line taking children through a compulsory curriculum where they pass their exams, move on to the next stage, pass their exams again and move on to the next stage (maybe university), pass their exams and get a certificate that they are educated or qualified.

An alternative way of thinking is to see education as the unfolding of a person, the development of individuals and groups in society, in which their potential begins to grow. It's like a flower opening up. From this perspective each child needs a different curriculum and different support for them to realise their full potential. There is no reason that this should start at three and finish at 18 or 21. The process can go on throughout life.

The current education system with schools, colleges, universities, all leading to formal qualifications, has been in existence for very long time. But it is not necessarily relevant for the future or for all people. In this book we are proposing the development of a learner-centred system alongside the existing system. The alternative system needs to be much more flexible. It needs to have the learner much more in the driving seat. If the current pandemic is just a harbinger of massive global disruption, accelerated by climate change, mass migration and economic collapse as well as disease, then we need an educational infrastructure that is aimed at freeing people to think critically and creatively, take initiatives and develop agency. We need a flexible system which will allow all sorts of possibilities, many of which have not yet been foreseen.

Part One examines how learner-centred educational systems, with alternative views of what learning really is, have been around for a very long time and show great possibilities.

EARLY EDUCATORS

Was Socrates guilty as charged[1]? Socrates died in 399 BC at the ripe old age of 71. He was a learned intellectual who campaigned for democracy[2]. He was forced to drink hemlock and die. What was his crime?

The charge sheet said he had practised 'impiety' *and* had 'corrupted the young'. His crime was hanging around in the marketplace and asking questions of anyone who was willing to listen. He had a view of education which involved asking questions, inviting people to examine their assumptions, seeing the consequences of a particular line of thought – in short what today is called 'critical thinking'. So why were the people of Athens so against him? By all accounts his trial followed due process, and it was a jury of 501 citizens who found him guilty. The context was years of disasters hitting Athens – plague, defeat by Sparta, civil unrest. Clearly the gods were angry and who was to blame? It must be the man who was asking too many questions and getting the youth to think. He *had* to go, and go he did. Did Socrates have a curriculum that he was trying to deliver to his pupils? On the contrary, he held that that wise teachers know that they know nothing and have nothing to impart. Their role is to help pupils discover truth for themselves. This may lead the pupils to seek out technical expertise or knowledge that can be transferred by another, from a builder, orator or shoemaker for example. But the education is based on dialogue and largely content free. One exception is that Socrates put virtues such as justice at the heart of good life; but his basic educational approach was to ask questions.[3]

Aristotle (384 – 322 BC) was also concerned with moral education. Indeed, educators throughout history have been preoccupied with general upbringing and the moral person as much as the development of knowledge and skills. Where Socrates focused on reason and dialogue, Aristotle held that knowledge is acquired inductively through experience and thought. The mind starts off empty and, from the moment of birth (or even before), the child is bombarded with information through the senses; the teacher's job is to help the learner organise and make sense of this manifold range of experiences.[4]

Ibn Sina (980 – 1037 AD) the mediaeval philosopher, known more in the west as Avicenna, was a Persian polymath and is seen as one of the most significant thinkers of Islam's golden age. He wrote a book chapter called *The Role of the Teacher in the Training and Upbringing of Children* as a guide to teachers working in schools attached to mosques. He emphasised the importance of group work and of manual education. He also developed the theory of the *tabula rasa*, the idea that the human intellect is a blank sheet at birth and that knowledge comes through experience from which universal concepts are abstracted.[5] These are developed through reasoning and further experience. He wrote about the intellect as being active. Ibn Sina merged the approaches of Socrates and Aristotle.

Ibn Tufail (1106 – 1185) was a Spanish Muslim philosopher, physician, mathematician and poet. He further developed the *tabula rasa* theory. He held that understanding is possible *without* the help of tradition and revelation – in modern terms we say it is possible to be an autodidact[6] or to be self-taught.

In later centuries we find philosophers such as Locke (1631 – 1704) and Rousseau (1712 – 1778) also holding that the mind of a child was a *tabula rasa*. For Rousseau the child was innately good and that anything bad that developed was the product of the child being immersed in an immoral society. Again, the source of knowledge was the senses. Rousseau stressed also the importance of active learning and how movement is crucial to the learning process. He believed in learning by doing.

These are a few examples of a deeply rooted educational tradition in which the learners are seen as the active agents, and the teacher's role is to help them learn. If the learners are following their own interests they are more likely to be motivated. If they are forced to follow a compulsory curriculum, and the quality of the learning experience is measured by or exams, then deep learning goes out of the window.

SCHOOLING, EDUCATION AND LEARNING

"Life is not linear, it's organic - we create our lives symbiotically as we explore our talents. We are obsessed with this linear narrative in education... A big issue is conformity... We have sold ourselves into a fast-food model of education and it is impoverishing our spirits and our energies as much as fast food is depleting our physical bodies ...

"We need to change metaphors. We have to move from an industrial model of education, a manufacturing model which is based on linearity, conformity and batching... We need to move to a model that is based on the principles of agriculture. We have to recognise that human flourishing is not a mechanical process, it's an organic process. You cannot predict the outcomes of human development. All you can do, like a farmer, is create the conditions under which they will begin to flourish..."

Sir Ken Robinson

Consider three concepts: *schooling*, *education* and *learning*. Current *schooling systems* are generally based in institutions – schools, colleges and universities. In most countries there are prescribed curricula and public exams. The 'success' of an institution is generally measured by student performance in these exams. Schooling is something that is largely done to young people. They attend institutions outside the home from the age of 4 or 6 to 16 or 18, depending on the laws of the land. Some then go on to higher education for another three or more years. During this time they take more tests and exams. At each transition point they receive some certification recording the level they have reached. Often this certification is a passport to going on to the next level. Inherent in the concept of a passport is that not everyone has the right to travel, only those who have the passport. It is a method of rationing scarce resources, even involving the deliberate creation of scarcity so that those who are 'qualified' are able to demand higher returns whether or not certification matches competence.

The word *education* is used loosely and in different ways by different people. It can apply to a system, an individual, a profession or a social phenomenon. Many people distinguish between *education* in the sense of an individual's open-ended development (Latin *educere – to bring out*) and *training* (Latin *trahere – to drag or pull*), in which a predetermined set of skills or knowledge is transferred from one person to another.

We want to focus on *learning* (Old English *leornian – to get knowledge, be cultivated, study, read, think about*). This emphasises what the learner does as an active, creative agent and not just a passive recipient of someone else's thoughts. There are connotations of upbringing, but within the context of taking responsibility for one's own thoughts and behaviour.

As Ken Robinson pointed out, schooling is currently a linear process based on an industrial model – one where students are processed in batches based on geography (itself loaded with inequality) and date of birth rather than ability and interest. Schools are locked institutions with learning driven by exams and regulated by timetables, curriculum and bells. This all conspires to frustrate real, deep education.

Yet most of what we learn is *not* through the schooling system. We learn from our parents, our siblings and peers, and above all through living and reflecting on all manner of experiences. We learn from others through discourse, listening, reading and watching. We learn from ourselves as we restructure our own thoughts in the light of new or contradictory experiences. And we learn throughout life. So why do we accept the status quo of a standardised curriculum?

The time has come to look for an alternative for schools. There is no consensus as to what phrases like 'improving schools' or 'learning more' actually mean. The words 'education', 'knowledge' and 'learning' are used carelessly as though everyone knows and agrees what they mean. They do not distinguish between 'education' and 'schooling'. If we value creativity and critical thinking the awful truth is that schools are getting worse as the demands of compulsory curricula become ever greater and inspection regimes' grip tightens. And this movement is world-wide.

A frightening experience

Twelve years ago I was in Astana, Kazakhstan in the government's curriculum centre with a group of technology teachers who were writing part of their new national curriculum for schools. My role was to advise on how design education could be integrated into the curriculum to replace a very traditional crafts-based subject called 'Labour Training'. The stated purpose was to develop a subject that enhanced school pupils' creativity. What might be learned from the British experience of Design & Technology as a school subject? The workshop was going well, and all were excited at the open-ended learning opportunities that this new subject offered.

Suddenly I was called away for a meeting at the Kazakhstan ministry of education. Present were the ministry's heads of curriculum, planning and finance. The minister had asked them to create a new curriculum and assessment regime that was affordable, and which would demonstrate year on year that schools were improving and that pupils were learning more. How did we approach this problem in the United Kingdom? I recall a deep unease – even sense of gloom – as I realised that across the world there must be similar discussions going on in ministries of education, parliaments and the media. Yet was this what pupils and their teachers, their parents and grandparents actually wanted? Was this insistence on performance, targets and measuring killing real education? If so, who was it benefitting?

James Pitt

The DHL model of curriculum

Most educational policy makers are locked into a mechanistic, linear model of education that is modelled on the production line. Children, batched by age, are compelled to enter the school system and are taught subjects by teachers who are charged to deliver a curriculum that has been approved by the government. Outputs are measured in some form of standardised testing and are deemed to be proportionate to the inputs – the quality and quantity of the teaching, the resources of the school buildings and equipment, and the efficiency of the whole institution and its constituent parts. Oh yes, and how hard the pupils apply themselves – but even then the unmotivated or disruptive pupil is seen to be the fault and hence responsibility of the school. Arguments rage about what should go into the curriculum, such as national history or world history, or at what age children should be introduced to Shakespeare or learn to make soup, what are the best class sizes, should teachers' pay depend on performance – all without standing back and asking, "What's it all about then?" Trying to make schools more efficient without asking what schools are for is the road to madness. The idea that a central authority can plan real education of children through defining what they must be taught, approving teaching materials and approaches, testing the children, rating the teachers and their schools in league tables is to deny these children myriad educational opportunities and inhibit their natural learning.

MORE HISTORICAL EXAMPLES

Let's return to history. Not everyone saw learning as something that could be prescribed, packaged and delivered. There have always been people with a more holistic attitude.

L'École Mutuelle

In the middle of the 18th century an enlightened educator, M. Herbault, established a Mutual School for poor children in Paris. Unlike traditional schools run by religious foundations in which pupils were instructed in groups, the mutual school relied on older or more skilful children to teach the less skilful. As children moved up the school they in turn became teachers as well as learners. This was cost-effective, as one teacher could supervise many more pupils at once than in a traditional class where the teacher presents the same thing to the whole group at the same time. A mutual school might have a large room with some hundreds of pupils supervised by a single teacher. The intermediate pupils worked both with the less advanced as teachers and with the more advanced as learners. There will always be a level that a child can slot into, though this might vary according the topic of study. This active and cooperative approach to learning enabled children to work at their own pace. The result was achieving basic literacy far more quickly than through conventional whole class teaching. As the Roman Stoic philosopher Seneca had said more than seventeen centuries earlier, "We learn by teaching" (Docendo discimus).

Mutual schools waxed and waned in popularity. They were attacked in 1824 by Pope Leo Xll who saw them as a threat to the social order. They were not being controlled nor regulated by central authority. What sorts of things were being learned or what attitudes developed? Ultra-Royalist forces led to the closure of many of the mutual schools, and the creation of a central ministry of public instruction in 1828. There was a short-lived resurgence after the July Revolution with 2,000 Ecoles Mutuelles running alongside the denominational schools, mainly in the cities where there were larger numbers of students. But in 1833 Minister of Education Francois Guizot decreed that control of elementary schools should be centralised or 'normalised'. They should be run in a similar way to those of religious societies such as the Christian Brothers, with whole-class, simultaneous instruction. To ensure that this happened he set up special colleges to control the training of teachers. Thus within a few years the mutual schools were marginalised in France[7].

Tolstoy (1828 – 1910)

Leo Tolstoy is well known for his novels and short stories; he is less well known for the alternative schools that he established and the educational principles that underpinned them[8]. Having decided to dedicate himself to farming and education, in 1859 Tolstoy established a school at Yasnaya Polyana, where he lived, for the children of local farmers. By 1863 there were 13 schools in the region following Tolstoy's approach. His literary friends were appalled, but Tolstoy said that the peasants were illiterate and therefore should be helped to read if only so that they could read his works.

Tolstoy was a kindred spirit of Rousseau in that he adopted ideas of individualism and emphasised the right of the child to develop in total freedom according to his or her own inherent personal characteristics. He believed that there is no other way to influence children except through an understanding of their mind, talents, characteristics and personalities. Children must be given freedom of movement and expression to explore their inner world in a spontaneous manner, through work and activity out of free choice. He assumed that children are good, curious, desiring to grow and abounding in the wish to be free.

For Tolstoy, education was an effort to bring forth and enrich the original spirit of the child. Education must be free, voluntary and accessible to all. Tolstoy opposed using any coercion in education, including the assumed right of government to impose a curriculum. He saw force as based upon arbitrary will. A child has their own truth, and one should not attempt to force adult truths upon them.

Tolstoy was against separating learning into disconnected subjects. School must remain an educational laboratory open to changes and contributions, renewing itself and developing in order not to hold back human advancement.

For Tolstoy, noise and chaos in school were the natural order of things. The principal task of the teacher was to listen and clarify what the students said– not to lecture – and there was no podium for the teacher. Pupils were free to enter and leave when they desired. There was a regular day with studies from 8am to 12pm, 3pm to 6pm, often continuing until 7pm by demand. The morning lessons were usually in reading, writing, grammar, drawing, music, maths, history, science and religion; in the afternoon there were physics experiments, lessons in singing, reading and writing. However, there was no fixed timetable – lessons were shortened, lengthened or cancelled relative to interest. On Saturdays, teachers met to discuss and plan for the following week. The teachers had a common diary in which to write of their failures and successes.

The Tolstoyan curriculum can be summarised as follows:

- There are no obligatory subjects

- A teacher should be flexible and ignore "coverage" of material or "completion" of a study plan

- Experiment and acquisition of experience are the focal points

- Every instruction ought to be only an answer to a question arising from the life of the learner

- There should be no material prescribed on the basis on convention or tradition

- Work need not be completed

- The curriculum need not be comprehensive

- There are no sacrosanct subjects everyone must learn

- The school is rooted in the life of the community so that everyone has a stake in it.

Teachers were free to teach in any manner they saw fit. There were no good or bad methods, just what was thought appropriate or inappropriate to the character of a child at that particular minute. Individualised learning was the key. The teacher should not try to surround the pupil with impervious walls against worldly influences;

the principal task was to make material meaningful to the pupil, inspire their motivation and bring them satisfaction from their studies. The teacher must accompany children through their free choices and encourage and nurture their enthusiasms. Ernest Howard Crosby, the American reformer and writer, summed up Tolstoy's contribution to education in these words[9]:

> *"The best environment for a child, and hence the best school, is the one which presents the widest range of selection for his activities, and which leaves the choice as far as possible to him. Whenever the school of the future begins to realize this ideal, the happy children of that day and the well-rounded men and women, full of energy and readiness, who will grow up from them, will owe a debt of gratitude to Count Tolstoy, for he will surely have his high place among the pioneers of a freer and truer education."*

Happy children? Wanting to learn? Now there's something we could aim for.

John Dewey (1859 – 1952)

Like Tolstoy, Dewey established his own elementary level school, which he called a Laboratory School, to develop and test his ideas. And like Tolstoy he saw the need for school to be an integral part of community life and for the learners to be the agents rather than passive recipients of their own learning. In 1907 he wrote:

"[We need to] make each one of our schools an embryonic community life, active with types of occupations that reflect the life of the larger society, and permeated throughout with the spirit of art, history, and science. When the school introduces and trains each child of society into membership within such a little community, saturating him with the spirit of service, and providing him with the instruments of effective self-direction, we shall have the deepest and best guarantee of a larger society which is worthy, lovely, and harmonious".[10]

Dewey emphasised the democratic, social and moral nature of the school at a time when a factory system of schooling was being adopted by school planners, inspired by the industrial model of efficiency. He believed that curriculum should be based on the actual interests of children, thereby bringing out the relationship between human knowledge and social experience. Educationalists Michael Apple and Kenneth Teitelbaum point out that Dewey criticised public schools on many counts: they ignored the lives and real interests of students; teachers used language that bore little relationship to students' experience; they overused tests for assessing students and based on these, sent them either in an academic or manual direction. Dewey argued that all students should have the same opportunities and that learning should be built on their knowledge and experience, their real lives, and not fragmented into subjects. [11]

Like Tolstoy, Dewey stressed the importance of basic occupations.

> "[Through] growing food, cooking, building a shelter, making clothing, creating stories and artwork children could be best initiated into moral social membership. They would be provided with opportunities to learn 'the instruments of effective self-direction', as well as a sensitivity toward social issues and the ability (including reading, writing and problem-solving skills) to act on them. In effect, the classroom was to embrace the kind of democratic community life, concern for human dignity, and scientific intelligence that was sought outside the school. The 'means' were in fact the 'ends'." (Apple and Teitelbaum 2001) [12]

In many ways Dewey presaged the ideas of 21st century thinkers like Sir Ken Robinson and the importance of real-life learning – see for example the research of Guy Claxton of the Centre for Real World Education. Dewey can be seen as the father of modern trans-disciplinary, real life, trial-and-error, project-based learning. His ideas were adopted in Russia after the revolution until the state realised that they were being too successful in growing creative, self-directed people; the Soviet government held that they were too challenging. They were reintroduced in post-16 education in the 1990s after the collapse of the Soviet Union[13], only to be discouraged again when Putin came to power.

> *"The most important attitude that can be formed is that of desire to go on learning."*
>
> *John Dewey*

Paulo Freire (1921 – 1997)

Paulo Freire, one of the most influential 20th Century thinkers in education worldwide, is less well-known in English speaking countries. Is this because his ideas are were too radical for mainstream educators? The titles of his seminal works display his progressive approach – *Education, the Practice of Freedom* in 1969, *Pedagogy of the Oppressed* and *Cultural Action for Freedom* in 1970, and *Education for Critical Consciousness* in 1973.

Freire asks if education is the teachers depositing knowledge in a student's mind in the same way that one might deposit money in a bank to be used as needed in the future? Or is it a creative collaboration in learning in which "knowledge emerges only through invention and re-invention, through the restless, impatient, continuing and hopeful inquiry men[14] pursue in the world, with the world and with each other." [15]

The banking model of education has ten defining characteristics:

- The teacher teaches and the students are taught

- The teacher knows everything and the student knows nothing

- The teacher thinks and the students are thought about

- The teacher talks and the students listen – meekly

- The teacher disciplines and the students are disciplined

- The teacher chooses and enforces their choice, and the students comply

- The teacher acts and the students have the illusion of acting through the action of the teacher

- The teacher chooses the programme content, and the students (who were not consulted) adapt to it

- The teacher confuses the authority of knowledge with their own professional authority, which they set in opposition to the freedom of the students

- The teacher is the subject or active agent in the learning process, while the pupils are passive objects.

This blunts people's critical consciousness and maintains them in a largely unthinking acceptance of the status quo. For Freire, banking education is

"... well suited to the purposes of the oppressors, whose tranquillity rests on how well men fit the world the oppressors have created, and how little they question it.

"The more completely the majority adapt to the purposes which the dominant minority prescribe for them (thereby depriving them of the right to their own purposes), the more easily the minority may continue to prescribe. The theory and practice of banking education serve this end quite efficiently. Verbalistic lessons, reading requirements, the methods for evaluating 'knowledge', the distance between the teacher and the taught, the criteria for promotion; everything in this ready-to-wear approach serves to obviate thinking."[16]

Although written over 50 years ago this resonates with the feelings of many parents and teachers today. A statutory curriculum, standardised testing and published league tables of schools' performances – not to mention payment of teachers by students' results – are antithetical to real education. Is it any surprise that the appeal of fundamentalism is growing?

Like Tolstoy and Dewey, Freire advocates an educational partnership in which the teachers are co-learners and the learners are co-teachers. The content of the learning is negotiated with the learner in the driving seat. There is no simple set of measurable outcomes for such liberating education as it never stops, but the educated person can be recognised by an openness, willingness to challenge, creativity, ability to learn through dialogue and debate and above all an active, on-going engagement in society to bring about a better world. These attributes are needed post-pandemic more than ever.

Ivan Illich (1926 – 2002)

Another giant of 20th century education is Ivan Illich, whose best-known book *Deschooling Society* also appeared in 1970. Illich hit the world of education with the alarming proposal that we need to get rid of schools, at least as we know them. In *Deschooling Society* he ponders how schooling – as distinct from education – has acquired such massive prestige and funding. He answers that the prestige comes from their divisive role in society and being a major means for preserving the status quo. He calls for the disestablishment of schools, and for a law "forbidding discrimination in hiring, voting or admission to centres of learning based on previous attendance at some curriculum."[17]

Although he wrote in the late 1960s and early 1970s, his critique of school is equally pertinent today. He opens chapter one on *Why We Must Disestablish School*:

"Many students, especially those who are poor, intuitively know what the schools do for them. They school them to confuse process and substance. Once these become blurred, a new logic is assumed: the more treatment there is, the better are the results; or, escalation leads to success. The pupil is thereby 'schooled' to confuse teaching with learning, grade advancement with education, a diploma with competence, and fluency with the ability to say something new. His imagination is 'schooled' to accept service in place of value. Medical treatment is mistaken for health care, social work for the improvement of community life, police protection for safety, military poise for national security, the rat race for productive work. Health, learning, dignity, independence and creative endeavour are defined as little more than the performance of the institutions which claim to serve these ends, and their improvement is made to depend on allocating more resources to the management of hospitals, schools and other agencies in question."[18]

As well as critiquing schooling and showing how much of the learners' experience is antithetical to real education, Illich proposed a better alternative. What is new in the 21st century is that we now have the technology to bring this alternative into being. This is what we explore in Part Three.

Illich starts with the premise that a good educational system should have three purposes. First, it should provide all who want to learn with access to resources at any time of their lives. Second, it should empower all who want to share what they know, to find those who want to learn it from them. Finally, it should furnish all those who want to present an issue to the public with the opportunity to make their challenge known.

Illich observed that every community is full of learning resources, especially in the experiences and wisdom of those in the community. Equally, every community is full of things that could be instrumental in learning. Suppose I want to learn Arabic. There will be some local speakers. Could I link up with them? Maybe if a few of us want to learn Arabic we could form a class, or a group for conversation. Or if I want to learn how to build a web site or deter the slugs in my vegetable patch, or if I am fascinated by astrophysics, medieval history, how to lay bricks or mend my iPad – there is bound to be someone who could teach me. In many cases I could learn on the job.

Illich proposed four types of well-resourced and well-managed learning networks in each neighbourhood or town, to which every citizen has access throughout life. These are:

- Reference services to educational objects – so that the learner can find what they need to learn from. Some will be in libraries, or rental agencies, laboratories or even workplaces such as factories, airports or theatres. Plant that is used in the daytime could be used for learning in the evenings

- Skill exchanges – through which people who have something specific to offer can link with those who want something

- Peer-matching – a communications network so that people can collaborate and find partners for their inquiries

- Reference services to educators-at-large – the professional educators who can advise, mentor both learners and (in the case of children) their parents and who can accompany learners on their journeys of discovery.

Illich's ideas are the inspiration of what we are proposing in Part Three. In Illich's vision there is no compulsory curriculum, at least beyond the basics such as listening, reading, thinking, writing and numeracy that can be found in primary schools. Someone who wants to pursue astrophysics will soon realise that they will need maths and possibly chemistry, philosophy and programming skills for building models. But they will learn these as a means to their chosen ends. Someone who wants to train as a joiner or heating engineer will be motivated to learn the functional English and maths to be able to do the job well. No longer does a learner follow a curriculum devised by bureaucrats or remote academics, let alone government ministers who are here today and gone tomorrow. Each learner develops their own, personalised curriculum with guidance from their mentors. And this continues throughout life.

If this scenario were to come about, some schools and colleges as we know them might become learning hubs or learning exchanges. Over time they will be greater in number, smaller and cheaper to maintain, as much learning will happen beyond the physical institution. We envisage that they would be more like community centres with maker labs, cafés, libraries, laboratories and spaces for performances. With the disappearance of the artificial distinction between 'practical' and 'academic' learning, and vocational skills being acquired largely on the job, many workplaces will also have learning areas. Education and training[19] become collaborative, community projects, often localised and responding with agility to changing local circumstances.

OTHER EXAMPLES OF REAL EDUCATION

There has been a tradition for over 2,000 years in western Europe (no doubt elsewhere as well) of a liberating education that encourages learners to think critically. It holds that there should be no division between learning and the rest of life, nor between the so-called 'practical' and 'academic'. It rests on the assumption that the learner is in the driving seat; the job of the teacher is to help that learner to realise their deeper purpose and grow into whom they want to be. There are many more such examples of learner-centred, liberating education, which we will give no more than a passing mention. You, the reader, can follow up on any of these.

Steiner-Waldorf schools have been around for over a hundred years. Their robust curricula based on the insights of Rudolf Steiner, and approach to learning in encouraging the unfolding of the child rather than stuffing them full of 'knowledge' has led to them being one of the fastest-growing educational movements worldwide, if not in the UK. There are now over 3,000 Steiner schools and kindergartens in 71 countries[20].

The Reggio Emilia schools in Italy show that creativity and collaboration can be at the heart of a school, and that traditional subjects can fit in around this quite naturally. Learning is holistic and fun, and students are not distracted by dividing knowledge into artificial subjects or silos.

The International Baccalaureate Organisation (IBO) requires that students working towards the IB Diploma produce an extended essay. This is an independent piece of self-directed research finishing with a 4,000-

word paper and usually an interview or *viva voce* with the student's supervisor. In many ways this is similar to the Extended Project Qualification offered by some UK exam boards. In these, the student also chooses a topic to investigate but the outcomes could be as wide as a research paper, a performance or production, or an artefact that they have designed and made. In these last two categories there must also be a written report including a production log. Teachers report that because the student has chosen their own topic or project there is a very high level of commitment. Often these provide the basis of an interview when the student applies for a job or university place.

Schools can run successfully with students taking a high level of responsibility including being on the governing body and appointing teachers, as in The Sands School in Devon.

The pandemic requires remote learning, and at last more educational institutions are using peer-to-peer and flipped learning strategies. Peer-to-peer recognises that students can naturally learn from each other, and that learning is intrinsically a social project. Flipped learning is when independent study is the normal way of acquiring knowledge, and discussion in class is to make sense of it and digest it. This is the opposite of the traditional model of the teacher giving knowledge in lessons or lectures, and homework or assignments are there to consolidate it.

Much progressive learning is through project work, often based on problem-solving. In negotiation with their tutors, students determine their own topics and the questions they want to explore. The role of the tutor is more that of mentor than giver of knowledge. This can be found at all levels from primary schools through to doctoral theses. Project-based learning is particularly well developed in areas like art or design & technology. Projects capture the interests of learners when they are rooted in their real-life interests. If the student is highly motivated they will go the extra mile and do it well. Many students can pick up real-life projects when they collaborate with businesses or indeed any institution outside the school. In the later years of current school- or college-based learning, experiences like this could be far more widely available.

The rapid expansion of home education, already growing before the pandemic, is opening some young learners to collaborate with their parents and other families in a community-based approach to learning.

Unfortunately, the prevalent trend in the mainstream is based on the ideas and mistaken epistemology of American philosopher E. D. Hirsch. He argues for prescriptive 'cultural literacy', a core body of knowledge[21] that every child should have. Although inspired by notions of equity – that every child has the right to 'their' culture – it operates within what Freire calls 'banking education'. This approach was made compulsory in England by Michael Gove. The philosophy underpinning it and the practice that follows serves to negate all the approaches to learning outlined above. The current regime in mainstream English schools (and many universities) is built on a compulsory, knowledge-based curriculum, assessed through standardised tests leading to schools being compared in league tables. It is likely to stop learners from thinking for themselves, and prevent development of their critical faculties and love of learning throughout life.

What's going on in schools today

Ask parents what they want from schools and they usually say they want their children to be happy, healthy, resilient and capable of thinking for themselves. They also want the schools to be vehicles for getting qualifications. But are these two aims compatible? Parents also say they want their children to be exposed to opportunities for learning new things. Actually, many parents want to get their children into prestigious universities and obtain well-paid jobs. Some parents aspire for their children to achieve positions of influence and power, whether it's in business or politics. Of course, this is only available to a small percentage and the private schools do it *par excellence.*

Yet almost all state schools are modelled on the private schools, and the league tables that are published focus on exam results. How about league tables that indicated happiness, critical thinking, inclusivity, solidarity and creativity? Schools perpetuate the lie that if you work hard, do well and move on to the next stage then you will get more out of life. Governments and exam boards maintain this myth, even when good exam results or degrees are no longer a passport to success.

The internet has accelerated the concentration of wealth into the pockets into a few company owners while stimulating an explosion in casual, gig-economy labour. Artificial intelligence is poised to transform the job market in ways we are only just beginning to fathom. It is likely that most people will not have jobs in future and that employment will be a succession of short-term contracts and regular career changes. The people who will flourish will be those who can be creative and flexible. Survey after survey finds employers saying they want school leavers to have soft skills of communication, functional numeracy, the flexibility to be proactive, resilience and creativity.

If this is what employers really want, they are not getting it from schools. Most state schools have cut back on creative activities like drama, music and design; it is the private schools (again) that provide best creative resources for pupils. It is interesting that some big employers no longer look for formal qualifications so much as a portfolio of life experiences showing how the applicant can put their hand to many different things. Schools are failing employers.

And what do pupils want? Who knows, as no one asks them? Or if they are consulted it is usually between limited, predetermined choices such as suggestions for school lunch menus. Schools do provide the opportunity for pupils to meet a wider selection of people, and this is rightly valued: the pandemic has shown the need for such community hubs. But pupils are not in the driving seat for curriculum design, teaching and learning.

Teachers have a raw deal. Head teachers identify the mental health of teachers as a huge problem as they struggle to make schools work. For the last six years recruitment targets have not been met, and many teachers are keen to leave the profession. Even before the pandemic we saw headlines in serious newspapers such as:

'Every lesson a battle': Why teachers are lining up to leave[22]

Burned out: Why are so many teachers quitting or off sick or with stress[23]

Teachers are leaving the profession in droves ... and little wonder. Who would want to be one in modern Britain?[24]

The pandemic has hugely increased stress on teachers. There is often discussion of paying teachers more to secure retention, especially in shortage subjects such as maths and science[25]. But this will not solve the problem; the root cause of teacher pain is that schools are being pushed into trying to achieve things for which there is no consensus. The pupils know it, the teachers know it and the government pretends that with some minor tweaks of money, employment conditions, inspection criteria and reporting, all will be well and staffing crises averted. This is simply not true. In 2018, 40% of teachers lasted less than five years in London[26] and in 2020 the Department for Education reported that almost one third had left the profession within five years of qualifying[27] .

PUPILS' MENTAL HEALTH

Even before the pandemic one in eight children in state schools have reported mental health problems. And the government says it is concerned about safeguarding!

The sad truth is that schools are modelled on prisons. There are locked doors to keep a physical barrier between the school and the outside world. In a sense it was always thus. Governments have always had a tendency to spy on citizens (or should we call them subjects?) and to use coercive measures to keep people under control. French philosopher Michel Foucault describes in *Discipline and Punish; the birth of the prison*, how the state uses different mechanisms to keep people in line. Starting with public torture and moving through punishment – still public as with chain gangs – and different sorts of supervised disciplinary regimes, we see the emergence of the prison system in the 18th and 19th centuries. Central to this is the idea that not all the prisoners are being watched all the time, but that at any one time individual prisoners do not know if *they* are being watched. Thus, they are led to discipline themselves. It is the same with education, says Foucault: "Every educational system is a political means of maintaining or of modifying the appropriation of discourse, with the knowledge and the powers it carries with it" [28]. Are the Ofsted inspections fundamentally a mechanism for teachers and governors to conform and discipline themselves?

Why is this happening?

Education is dumbing us down

Most schools are bad for most people. They are *worse* than a waste of money, money which could be used towards liberating the human spirit and helping people have fulfilling lives. As John Taylor Gatto[29] said so eloquently, there are seven lessons that are taught in pretty well every school.

Lesson one: schools generate confusion which is "thrust upon kids by too many strange adults, each working alone with the thinnest relationship with each other, pretending, for the most part, to an expertise they do not possess". Children are required to learn disconnected facts with bells and classroom shifts that are bound to fragment understanding and inhibit the generation of meaning. School sequences are crazy, he says. On top of this "few teachers would dare to teach the tools whereby the dogmas of a school or a teacher could be criticised, since everything must be accepted." It is little wonder that systems thinking or attempting to take an holistic view of anything is not on the official curriculum.

The second lesson is class position. Learners are continually measured and given a number or ranking. "Numbering children is a big and very profitable undertaking, though what this strategy is designed to accomplish is elusive" says Gatto. When you think about it, it is not elusive. Together with testing against a rigid curriculum it is designed to generate lack of critical thinking and to encourage conformity. Giving learners a number serves to pigeonhole learners into academic successes or failures, thereby priming them psychologically for either well-paid or low-paid jobs.

The third lesson is to generate indifference. Yes we know that committed and noble teachers yearn to share their passion for the understanding that history can bring, or the elegance and beauty of mathematics, and occasionally they manage to do this. But fragmentation into subjects and a compulsory curriculum that uses bells to regulate learning time is quite simply counter-educational.

Lesson four is to generate emotional dependency. "By stars and red checks, smiles and frowns, prizes, honours and disgraces I teach kids to surrender their will to the predestinated chain of command." Children are encouraged to please their teacher. What would happen, one wonders, if the Universal Declaration of Human Rights was to apply to schools, let alone the UN Convention of the Rights of the Child[30] which talks of freedoms of expression, thought, and the right to privacy and association?

The fifth lesson is intellectual dependency. "Good students wait for a teacher to tell them what to do. This is the most important lesson of them all: we must wait for other people, better trained than ourselves, to make the meanings of our lives." Children who question the value of what they are being taught are deemed to be bad, naughty, irresponsible or disruptive. Parents, who have been well schooled in these same principles, are more likely to side with the school than with their offspring.

Lesson six is that self-esteem is provisional. Children are taught that what really matters is the grade they are achieving, rather than feeling good about learning something of their choice for the sheer love of it.

Finally, children are taught that *they cannot hide from all this*. Nor can teachers, who are also subject to constant assessments. Nor can schools, which are inspected or judged by their performance in public examinations. This creates terrible, dehumanising pressures under which teachers labour.

John Taylor Gatto argues, quite simply, that the purpose of the school system is to dumb most people down.

The Italian philosopher Antonio Gramsci looked at the power of authorities to shape people's perception, thinking and behaviour. Key mechanisms for control are schools and religions, far easier to manage than dealing with insurrection; it is only when these cultural institutions fail that the police and army are needed. Gramsci talks in terms of hegemony. Barry Burke explains how this can be seen as the organising principles of the ways we understand the world, or the metaphors that serve to determine our consciousness. What is taken as common-sense, the widely accepted attitudes, the beliefs about what is right and wrong and the values we live by are all rolled into this concept of hegemony. They permeate our lives, and in this way the dominant elites determine what seems natural, making people reluctant to challenge the status quo or examine power relationships too closely. [31]

Bryan Caplan says in *The Case Against Education – why the Education System is a Waste of Time and Money* that individuals and society would be better served by *less* schooling. Writing as an economist, he describes how pretty well everything one learns at school is quickly forgotten and useless anyway. So why is it, he asks, that people with higher degrees are paid more and keep their jobs for longer? Bryan Caplan says it is all to do with signalling. A student works hard, passes exams at school, goes on to a prestigious university, gets a good degree and then a higher degree. With this background the student approaches an employer, looking for a job. The employer is impressed but it is not because of the knowledge the applicant has accrued on their journey – most of it is irrelevant. What the employer likes is that the applicant has demonstrated that they are bright, hard-working and conformist. It is these qualities that success in formal education can flag up.[32]

Sadly, we agree.

So as more people get degrees, you need to get a higher degree to get ahead in the job market. As more people get a masters degree, you need a doctorate. Charles Chu says this is like people standing up at a football match. The person in front of you stands up, so you have to do so to see. Then so does the person behind you. By the time everyone in the stadium is standing up no one has a better view than before. Of course, there are other, non-economic benefits from learning. But we don't need a whole system devoted to promoting stupidity – lack of critical thinking or systems thinking – and conformity for people to achieve these.

Is it time for a change?

For years, governments across the world have been driving schools towards a narrow, compulsory curriculum and standardised or even tick-box testing at the expense of real education. It is not what students want, it is not parents want, it is not what teachers want, it is not what business wants. It is having a bad effect on the health of many children and older learners, and their teachers and lecturers. It fails to equip learners with the tools for an unknown future.

Yet learning is a natural, social activity that goes on throughout life. Learners can take responsibility for their learning; learning institutions can be run on a democratic basis. Curriculum can be personal and negotiated, and not compulsory. We have noted that peer-to-peer learning works and often the best teachers are other learners. Digital technologies offer unprecedented learning opportunities. Flipped learning, where students acquire information out of class and use teacher contact time to review and deepen it, could become the norm. Project-based learning motivates and inspires, especially when it is rooted in real-life contexts and challenges; there is no need to have a barrier between what goes on in a learning institution and the rest of a person's life.

The current emphasis on knowledge is both debilitating and counter-productive. Exams do not give a satisfactory picture of a student's skills and general aptitudes and can be a waste of time and money. Teachers at all levels are seriously demotivated by teaching to the test, which is leading to a crisis in education.

The pandemic is shaking everything and there are great new possibilities. What might an evolving 21st century education system look like? On what principles should it be based? What is the big picture?

PART TWO – THE STATE OF THE WORLD TODAY

INTRODUCTION

*P*art Two is about society; it examines the social and political context of education today. In Part One we looked at a few major educational thinkers and in Part Three will offer a way forward for recovering real learning. You, the reader, might ask "Do we really need a whole section on politics and economics in a book about education?"

We think it is essential. The shape of education today has been forged by same forces that led up to the 2008 financial crisis and the choice of austerity to shore up the global economic system. Formal education has always been highly politicised. This is more than governments wanting to make their mark when they get into power. The post-war consensus that was rooted in the belief that governments should manage demand to maintain full employment (so called Keynesian economics) This has been replaced by the market-driven beliefs of Hayek and Friedman (described as neo-liberals): that the problem was lack of competition, too much government interference, and that managing demand only led to rising prices and labour unrest. The so-called winter of discontent in 1978/9 is claimed as an illustration of this failure.

Linked to this was suppression of the freer, open educational directions of the 1960s and 1970s that gave more autonomy to teachers, schools and local education authorities. In its place we have commodification and a culture of conformity in which the state sets out performance criteria and then providers compete to deliver at the lowest cost. For example, academy trusts are supposed to be more efficient and market-orientated.

If we ever are to challenge centralised control and return learning to learners, we need to understand some of the forces and new possibilities. Hitler gave the world a terrible warning when he said that whoever has the youth has the future. By contrast, Nelson Mandela said, "Education is the most powerful weapon which you can use to change the world."

Simply changing the infrastructure of education will not be enough to meet future challenges. We need to look at the wider economic and social forces and the possibilities of renewing society from the bottom upwards.

This is also a basis of hope. Much spiritual wisdom rests on the idea that good and bad, dark and light, progress and regress are interlinked. The Zohar for example, a foundation of Jewish mystical thought, holds that "There is no light except that which issues forth from darkness ... and no true good except that it proceed from evil" [33]. This thinking is found in many cultures. The bleakness of the present can be a sign of better things to come.

The future of the world looks uncertain and is depressing for many. What might happen if we get back to business as usual after Covid-19? What might give us hope and inspire a different economy and more humanised relationships? Part Three deals with the sorts of education might we need in either scenario.

> *"Machines which ape people are tending to encroach on every aspect of people's lives, and such machines force people to behave like machines."*
>
> *Ivan Illich*

BUSINESS AS USUAL

Climate change

Climate change is happening in real time. We can only guess at the longer-term effects of global warming as tipping points are reached and the consequences are out of all proportion to the marginal changes that precipitate them. Already there are droughts and famines, threats of food scarcity and more severe weather patterns. This demands an education that encourages curiosity, creativity and a willingness to embrace change.

Mass migration and populism

In 2015 some 244 million people lived outside their country of origin; mostly 'economic migrants' seeking a better life elsewhere[34]. There are no accurate figures for the number of people on the move today but already there are millions in North Africa who are, in the main, trying to enter Europe. As the climate of southern Europe becomes inhospitable there will be tens or even hundreds of millions of people on the move. That is without wars. This demands education for empathy and resilience. Without learning that is intrinsically social, there is a danger that people in Europe will respond with increased racism and xenophobia. The development of critical thinking in the population at large is the best prophylactic against populist demagogues running amok.

Disease

The Covid pandemic was predicted but no one was certain when it would come, nor what the consequences would be. Most governments chose not to prepare in advance despite the pandemics in the 20th and early 21st centuries. As habitats are destroyed and wildlife increasingly comes into contact with humans, such pandemics will happen more frequently. Climate change will exacerbate this. There will be more pandemics. This demands education for social responsibility.

Artificial intelligence, fewer jobs and the changing nature of work

Artificial intelligence and the changing nature of work are another trigger for massive structural disruption. Most commercial drivers will be replaced by driverless vehicles within the next twenty to thirty years. Already insurance companies, health care, law offices, retail and logistics are losing jobs to robots or algorithms that can provide a more reliable service than the people they replace. Work that has to be done on site such as building is giving way to pre-manufactured components that are assembled on site. 3D printing is becoming cheap and widely available. The old social contract of studying hard, getting qualifications, landing a job and having a career has disappeared for many people as we move towards zero hours contracts and a hand-to-mouth economy. The Bank of England has predicted that some 15 million jobs will disappear over the next ten years and whole professions be hollowed out, hitting in particular the middle class and low paid[35].

Plunder of the Commons

There is the plunder of the commons, where assets move from public to private ownership. It was not just the various enclosure acts that created legal property rights to land that was previously held in common. Land and parks, public buildings and utilities, libraries, schools, health centres, state-run services and social amenities generally that have been built or bought at public expense continue to be sold off, commodified and commercialised. Public authorities often take on the risks of a development whilst the private sector benefits from profits that accrue. This is a denial of opportunity for the majority.

"How can you buy or sell the sky, the warmth of the land? The idea is strange to us. If we do not own the freshness of the air and the sparkle of the water, how can you buy them? Every part of the Earth is sacred to my people. Every shining pine needle, every sandy shore, every mist in the dark woods, every clear and humming insect is holy in the memory and experience of my people. The perfumed flowers are our sisters, the deer, the horse, the great eagle, these are our brothers. The rocky crests, the juices in the meadows, the body heat of the pony, and the man, all belong to the same family."

Chief Seattle (1786 – 1866)

Democracy at risk

Representative democracy – "the worst form of government, except for all the others" as Winston Churchill put it – relies on a social contract. People chose representatives who make decisions on behalf of the people, until a new election. Effective democracy demands that people have a chance to be properly informed, or at least have access to truth. This requires freedom of information and the public exposure of 'fake news'. But above all it demands education to think critically.

Social media are manipulated to build a false common wisdom. Increasingly politicians can make outrageous claims and get away with it. Covid has exacerbated this as governments assume emergency powers and rule by decree.

Electoral systems that are not proportionate allow governments with minority support to control parliament – Boris Johnson had less than 30% of the electorate actually voting for his party and less than 45% of votes cast in his favour. Yet his majority in parliament was 80. Prime ministers can, and do, stuff the House of Lords with unaccountable supporters. Government at all levels is susceptible to professional lobbying. Local authorities have been drained of power and cash. This all conspires to enhance apathy or anger and reinforce a sense of powerlessness rather than agency. Directly elected mayors of regional authorities are a welcome move in the other direction, and yet their powers are contained by national policies. We need education that builds a sense of agency.

The changing economic context

After the Second World War there was a consensus in the West that governments had a role in rebuilding economies and in particular to maintain a high level of employment. Keynesianism – the adjustment of overall demand to maintain full employment – was broadly accepted. The state expanded into running everything from health provision, the transport infrastructure such as docks, airlines and railways. Educational institutions blossomed. Demand could be increased by state intervention in anything from the provision of housing to subsidising the film industry[36]. Jobs flourished in these expansions with the need for many intermediaries between consumer and supplier. Public money was being spent and state institutions needed to be monitored at all levels to see that money was being well spent, creating yet more jobs in inspection and accountability. In education there was a continuing rise in the number of teachers, inspectors and local authority advisers, not to mention providers of ancillary services such as educational psychologists, speech therapists, curriculum developers, teacher trainers and textbook writers.

Since the mid-1970s this trend has reversed. The trigger was rising wages and prices but limited growth. The economic framing of Hayek and Freidman began to replace that of Keynes and the dominant problem was now seen as inflation rather than the need for full employment. It was accepted that unemployment would rise as the government concentrated on keeping prices down, but new entrepreneurial and more efficient businesses would compensate with new jobs over time.

The state was now seen as causing problems in society rather than contributing to their solution. It looked only sensible to cut jobs in public service. This was the era of neo-liberalism and globalisation, characterised by the 'financialisaton' and privatisation of the public sector. Margaret Thatcher may or may not have actually said "A man who, beyond the age of 26, finds himself on a bus can count himself as a failure", but this sentiment expresses the spirit of that age. So did her comment, "Society? There is no such thing! There are individual men and women".

Tony Blair further developed this phase of post-war thinking but with a different slant. He poured money into the health service and education, thus expanding the number of jobs, assuming that profits and taxes from the growing finance sector would fund it. Yet he continued to champion the cause of globalisation and the marketization of public services. In his speech to the 2005 Labour Party conference[37] he called explicitly for more competition in health and education. The new jobs he helped to create were not to be controlled by the public.

The growth of debt

Some people began to question the wisdom of rolling back the state and encouraging unregulated markets. Whilst the finance system was being let go there was no parallel rise in wages; real wages were going down. Many jobs were being moved abroad. How could people be encouraged to keep spending? The mechanism was to encourage the growth of private debt. Education supported this with its focus on individual achievement, linked in people's minds with consumption. For many this was underwritten by the upward trend in house prices. The global expansion of private debt meant that the 2008 crash was inevitable. This ushered in the third phase of the post-war settlement which led to the rise of the precariat.

The emergence of the precariat

Nothing fundamentally changed in the aftermath of the 2008 crash. Some people continue to be in well-paid jobs with career prospects. Those who are set up for life can be called the 'salariat' in distinction to the 'precariat', a term made popular by Guy Standing in his 2011 book *The Precariat – the New Dangerous Class.*

Standing says that the precariat has grown out of the failures of globalisation and international capitalism and the ideological commitments of neo-liberalism – the rolling back of public service and dismantling of the institutions of social solidarity, whether they be trade unions or professional guilds, the district hospital or local school. Everything was commodified so that labour could be bought and sold. Firms were dismantled and turned into commodities and the most profitable bits transferred to huge holding companies, often registered off-shore or in low-tax havens. At the same time globalisation has potentially increased the workforce by some two billion as people can now work remotely, in effect migrating with their labour without having to move physically. It is little wonder that there has been a downward pressure on real wages over the last thirty years.

A new global class structure

There is a new global class structure. At the top there is the rentier plutocracy, the very few people who own most of the world's assets. Interestingly, intellectual property is now amongst the most valuable assets, either in the form of patents or copyright. Next there are the professional and managerial elites, usually grouped around the metropolitan centres. This group is reasonably secure with inherited wealth, sustainable jobs, pensions and being members of networks with other people from their class.

Then there is the broader salariat, comprised of people on permanent contracts. This group is being shrunk through short-term contracts and outsourcing. Academia provides a clear example of this with some highly prestigious Russell Group universities having well over half their staff on limited contracts or hourly rates of pay, described as "a reserve army of precarious and insecure and exploited labour" [38]. Many universities are hacking up teaching jobs into ever smaller bits and shoving people on to the worst contract they can get away with. Salaried professionals across all industries are expected to read emails that arrive when they are at home or even on holiday, or to work late to meet a deadline. The life of the salariat is becoming increasingly precarious.

The next group down can be called the proletariat or traditional skilled working class. This too is shrinking in the UK as manufacturing is outsourced or moved overseas to countries where labour is cheaper, or as a result of new technologies. It is hard to believe now that the print unions once represented a traditional class of craftsmen that had the industrial strength to hold newspaper owners to account.

Finally, there is the precariat, the massively expanding group of people in every country. They have a fundamental insecurity arising from unstable employment. They have no occupation narrative as in "I am a structural engineer", nor lifelong corporate narrative as in "I am the man from the Prudential" and no clear job trajectory. They have to do a lot of work in their free time that is unpaid and largely unrecognised.

Guy Standing talks of the 'precariatised mind' in which people accept this fragility and have to use much creative energy to survive. Their level of education is often higher than the work they are doing – arts graduates working as baristas, casual staff employed at events or qualified part-time staff on a zero-hours contract at a care home. Usually there is neither pension scheme, nor sick pay, and sometimes they have to fight for the limited holiday pay that is their right. Because they might rely on state benefits to supplement their income, many are caught in poverty traps where a little extra work might result in an 80% marginal tax rate, and often suffer huge problems if their benefits are suspended while something is worked out or if the claimant is sanctioned.

The precariat person is often forced into short-term and hence expensive debt to survive. The loans that university students are forced to take out put many in a precarious position; they become denizens more than citizens. They might have legal rights for example on conditions of work but are unable to enforce them.

Standing's analysis is supported by the Great British Class Survey of 2013, an empirical study which identified seven classes that exist in Britain, looking at economic, social and cultural capital[39].

The neo-liberal myth

Belief in free and efficient market forces has largely diminished, displaced by acceptance of rentier capitalism – 'the belief in economic practices of monopolization of access to any (physical, financial, intellectual, etc.) kind of property, and gaining significant amounts of profit without contribution to society'[40] . This was inevitable as the neo-liberal ideology was based on lies.

There never was a free market economy – it was hedged around by governments and international institutions such as the UN and its specialised agencies, ILO, UNCTAD, WTO, TRIPS (Agreement on the Trade Related Aspects of Intellectual Property Rights), and TRIPS' successor, the all-powerful WIPO (World Intellectual Property Organisation). Patents run for 20 years with an extra 20 years for pharmaceutical products, despite the fact that the original research was often funded in the state sector. Standing reckons the value of patents is some $20 trillion. Big corporations such as Google hoover up patents by buying up smaller companies such as Motorola to increase their economic rents. This is hardly a free and fair market, rather a free for all where there is no pretence of equal power or access.

There is the rise of trade agreements such as TPP, TTIP and CETA, which allow companies to sue governments for putative loss of earnings resulting from the latter having placed restrictions on the former's ability to trade freely. These trade agreements are often subject to Investor-State Dispute Settlement procedures (known as ISDS), which many see as favouring the big companies over democratically elected governments[41]. There are well over 3,200 international trade agreements that have locked up the global economy through ISDS mechanisms.

There is a plague of subsidies in almost every country, subsidies that are usually disguised. Things like working tax credits allow employers to pay less than the living wage, thereby bolstering the companies' rent-seeking capacity. Housing benefit allows private landlords to charge higher rents and the state pays a subsidy to the tenant; in reality the subsidy is a cash gift to the landlord which is processed via the tenant. There are all sorts of other subsidy mechanisms such as government grants, loans, buying of shares and tax credits and reliefs for companies, which are essentially public subsidies paid for by the public but which benefit the shareholders[42]. Often these are neither efficient, effective nor transparent[43].

Subsidies are used to encourage the development of particular technologies or to make intrinsically expensive supply systems appear financially competitive. For example, the UK government subsidises electricity from nuclear sources while cutting support for renewables[44]. The Equality Trust calculated that transport sub-sidies benefit the richest 10% three times more than the poorest 10%.[45] Corporate Welfare Watch calculates that subsidies to business were in excess of £90bn per year before the extra for Covid[46]. Note that this corporate welfare largely benefits big business.

There are further subsidies, such as state-funded research in universities leading to patents taken up by private companies or intellectual property being owned by commercial publishers. Doctors and nurses are trained in hospitals and then work in private practice. The massive physical, economic and social infrastruc-tures that have been built from public funds are used disproportionately by the better off.

Taxes foregone or subsidies of the kind illustrated have a knock-on effect on the public purse, as does the skewed allocation of the benefits accruing to the public infra-structure. Globalisation has weakened returns to labour in wages as manufacturing has gone abroad, only to be replaced by lower skilled service or administrative jobs here. Many of these workers are drawing on benefits as 'working poor'.

Overall, the returns of rising productivity have gone to capital and not in increased wages. This began in the mid 1980s and has accelerated since 2008. A combination of depressed wages, corporate subsidies, the skewed allocation of financial benefits from automation and new technology, plus the shock of the 2008 crash, has led to a breakdown of the post war social contract. Rising public sector debt – a large part of which was incurred by saving the banks and propping up asset prices – has led to calls for 'austerity' to 'balance the books'. This further punishes significant communities[47].

When people challenge what is claimed to be economic common sense and say that austerity is not the answer, mainstream neo-liberals retort, "Work is the best route out of poverty – so take it!" Despite the promise that wages will go up with more employment, higher productivity and greater profits, the opposite has happened.

How has our education system bred so many people who accept this as truth? It is clear that the traditional economic models no longer apply, yet the response from educators is still based on business as usual. Many want to stick to an education based on conformity, with what we think we know.

The economy and social cohesion

The world economy is intrinsically unstable. A 2019 IMF report quoted a 2016 study suggesting that an estimated $36 trillion of assets were being kept out of circulation offshore by individuals. This comes on top of nearly $3 trillion held offshore by corporations[48]. By definition, money hidden offshore cannot be counted accurately. Financial circuits are becoming fragmented and money does not flow around creating jobs and sustainable consumption. This happened in the Great Depression of the 1930s, but Roosevelt's New Deal mitigated the effects. The application of Keynes' theories about increasing government spending and lowering taxation to stimulate demand helped to pull the world out of recession, although it took the lead up to war to really make the point.

It was recognised even then that there was a flaw in the system and that in time – 30 years on, as it transpired – an inflationary wages and prices spiral might develop. As Kalecki noted[49], people learned how to game the system knowing that governments would always step in to preserve employment and try to deal with inflation. The oil shocks of the 1970s didn't help. The first signs of globalisation were already showing that national economies were increasingly a thing of the past.

The money circuits broke down in the late 1970s and Margaret Thatcher recognised that the social mood was ready for a flip. The priority was said to be stable prices, but it was essentially a political project too; many of its protagonists from the end of the 1950s were deeply averse to the rise of the democratic impulse and human rights, feminism, ecological and anti-war sensibilities.

The new clothes so carefully displayed promoted individualism, a freeing up of the financial sector, the mechanism of free-for-all markets (but not free and fair to all) to regulate supply and demand, cuts in taxation for the 'wealth creators' and cuts in social security spending for the 'shirkers'.

All of this was a kind of reboot. Capitalism had its own trajectory, eventually leading to the increase in private debt, financial instability and financial crisis of 2008. By default, formal education continued to underpin rather than challenge this, as no economic literacy was taught and the neoliberal myths remain unexamined.

The 2008 crash

In 2008, governments had the choice of saving the banks or saving the economy. Obama in the USA saved the banks. The UK government response was also to save the banks by nationalising the banks' liabilities and introducing quantitative easing, which was essentially more government-backed credit. But this did not go to the person in the street. It did not produce a healthy circulation of money. Once again there has been a one-way flow into asset accumulation in such things as house prices and shares. And the people who own the assets will try not to let it change.

While the banks had been saved by the government's taking on and nationalising private debt, the government promised to cut back on public expenditure in order to maintain some credibility. Using an inappropriate metaphor[50] of family budgets ("You cannot spend more than you have coming in") they imposed austerity measures. Government spending was cut, combined with tax cuts for the well-off. Many people are now worse off, and public services from health to social care to buses are being drained of cash.

But the underlying problem remains, in that big business still needs people to buy its products. If most people have a reduced disposable income they are less likely to spend. Once again there is a dangerous rise in private debt. The irony of the 2008 crash is that the banks caused it, yet austerity measures were imposed to save the banks. Rather than using the metaphor of family budgets we could have used the language of investment and, if it is not too radical for middle England, to ask how to invest in the commons.

Some in the ever-expanding precariat stick part of the blame onto the salariat such as teachers, health workers, bureaucrats and indeed anyone who appears to have a secure job and decent pension. Many worse-off do not blame the rich who are hidden from view, or because they aspire to be part of the rich, or because super-rich celebrities are idolised by the media. The myth that anyone can make it is steadily promulgated despite evidence to the contrary. Education has helped to maintain this myth with its focus on individual achievement and a decontextualized curriculum.

After all it is the elites who are currently in control of the framing (in the words of George Lakoff) – that is the language that people use to think about things and hence the lenses through which people view or perceive the world, the metaphors by which people think and live. The dominant framing is socially divisive. This is why liberating approaches to education outlined in Part One find little favour with the elites, except in private schools.

To borrow a concept from Antonio Gramsci, the organic intellectuals of the right – the creative thinkers who are shaping common sense – have been in the driving seat. One of the most penetrating insights on the rise of Trump and support for Brexit comes from Christophe Guilluy, who has studied gentrification in French cities and charted how those who feel left behind are likely to move to the right[51]. This resonates with David Goodhart's distinction between 'anywhere' people for whom the world is their oyster and 'somewhere people' who feel more rooted geographically[52]. The anywhere people are better educated in the formal sense, richer, better networked and mobile, and able to make the most of what is on offer. For them it is self-evident that freedom of movement is desirable. By contrast the somewhere people are more likely to feel resentment if their town or neighbourhood is taken over by outsiders and prone to blame the incomers. There is a real danger that towns, cities and countries become increasingly divided, leading to serious social unrest. Our current educational system is exacerbating this as the precariat expands in size whilst seeing their life choices diminished.

How might educators respond to Business as Usual?

If there was ever a time for a progressive alliance to develop a new narrative that challenges the dominant worldview, it is now. Real education must play a part in this. Yet this is not happening. The left either throws up its hands in despair, blaming anyone but themselves for rising ignorance and racism, or it retreats in confusion from the political and economic process and fights internal fights.

State education is partly to blame for this. The curriculum and approach to teaching in most schools and universities have been so standardised and dumbed down that the development of critical thinking has all but disappeared as a policy objective, if indeed it was ever there for the population as a whole. The near-total lack of any kind of systems thinking leads to simplistic, linear cause-and-effect analyses such as 'Those Romanians are taking my job!' or 'People voted for Brexit because they were too stupid to see that they were being deceived!' Our compulsory education has left most people with little sense of agency, feeling that they cannot change things, and hence angry.

What sorts of attitudes, knowledge and skills will enable people to cope, let alone thrive, in this new world? Business as usual means people frightened of climate change and disease, unable to buy a house or find secure accommodation or employment, frustrated by not being able to do what they want to do and crippled by debt which holds them in fear. In this scenario we need education for sociability, empathy, critical thinking, flexibility, communication and inquiry and above all resilience. We can leave the accumulation of knowledge *per se* to enthusiasts and hobbyists – and to the machines!

We are in a radically new situation in which jobs in the middle are being hollowed out. Elites will always be there, largely metropolitan with a disproportionate number of graduates from high-status universities. The established middle class also has a high proportion of graduates, mainly in the arts and humanities, and the technical middle class has a high proportion of graduates from the STEM (science, technology, engineering and maths) subjects. There is an emerging group of new affluent workers who are young and socially active. This group does not have a high proportion of graduates, and nor does the traditional working class which is shrinking. Service industries have a higher proportion of graduates, mainly from the arts and humanities. It seems that our current educational model is geared almost entirely to meeting the needs of the rentier plutocracy, the professional and managerial elites, and the salariat on permanent contracts. Together these represent just over one third of the population, and even there, many jobs will soon be replaced by artificial intelligence.

Yet still, parents are persuaded that the best chance for their children is to aim for the elites, established or new middle class. The current regime of working hard for GCSEs, A levels, first and second degrees and getting good grades throughout is designed to select people for this. The bitter truth is that there will not be enough jobs.

Ironically, industry and commerce continue to demand a different approach from within the mainstream. In March 2018 Paul Dreschler, the President of the CBI, called for less emphasis on rote learning and exam results, and more on developing a spirit of enquiry that enables people to shape the future as well as cope with the present workplace[53]. The Times Educational Supplement reported[54] a growing consensus that the current knowledge-based curriculum is too narrow. "Attainment is not enough", CBI education chief Neil Carberry is reported as saying: "There's a lot of support for the aims of Whole Education in the business community", arguing for skills development in parallel with knowledge. Business leaders do not accept that schools should have to choose between knowledge and skills in their curriculum planning. Both must be developed if young people are to be prepared both for work and for life in general.

> *"Schooling, which we engage in and which supposedly creates equal opportunities, has become the unique, never-before-attempted way of dividing the whole society into classes. Everybody knows at which level of his twelve or sixteen years of schooling he has dropped out, and in addition knows what price tag is attached to the higher schooling he has gotten. It's a history of degrading the majority of people."*
>
> **Ivan Illich**

A BETTER VISION

That all makes for depressing reading. But there are increasing signs of people doing things differently.

Life in towns and cities

Future gazing is a hazardous art at best, yet there is a convergence around a picture of a city or town in which people have more time, more challenges and more fun – but less disposable income. One such scenario is drawn by Kevin Carson[55]. This contains a feast of case studies of community initiatives that work. He sees city life revolving around community facilities such as open cafes, maker-labs or fab-labs, urban farms and community-supported agriculture.

The new city will be based on a radically different economic model with widely decentralised production and organisation. The state will be more of a platform (or series of platforms) to enable people to organise and meet their needs through networking and collaboration. Co-operatives of all sorts will be the basic institutions.

The Global Ecovillage Network or GEN provides many practical examples of co-operative living from around the world[56]. These vary from community organised solar power in India to developing a multi-generational collaborative housing scheme in New York. Many of these examples have a strong spiritual foundation – that is spiritual, not religious – and the common factor is respect and mutuality.

A community initiative in Athens saw residents of Vyronas repossess an abandoned municipal building to prevent it being privatised. It became a centre for education at all levels and was supported by a commons-friendly city government. One thing that came out of it is SynAthina, an online space with over 4,000 citizens' groups among its participants. Run by the City of Athens, it acts as a platform through which groups can co-ordinate and provides a listening post for identifying priorities for the city. It generates a new 'relationship between civic society and local governance and cultivates their dynamic, bidirectional bond'[57]. The spirit of this is co-creation, rather than the authority providing a service to the public [58].

Carson writes of the Partner State as an underpinning for such developments "not so much a 'government' as a system of *governance*. It need not be a state at all, in the sense of an institution which claims the sole right to initiate force in a given territory. It is, essentially, a nonstate social association—or support platform—for managing the commons, extended to an entire geographical region."

Another example is the Poblenou area of Barcelona where the authority provides infrastructure support for a new type of development, the Barcelona Digital

City[59]. This brings together the local fab labs or maker movement workshops, app developers and other software developers around a commitment to open, citizen-based development. They describe this approach as an open-digitalisation programme with "…free software and agile implementation of Barcelona City Council services that defines the process of profound, progressive change in the way the city will offer its services to the general public in coming years."

The Maker District pilot project in Poblenou "is based on a prototype of a productive and scalable city, which aims to contribute to the city's reindustrialisation through activities and projects that promote interaction between local communities and citizen initiatives, while also being linked to a global community."[60] New employment is generated: "Digital social innovation is fostered through the use of open technologies to combat societal challenges, and aims to enable a community of workshops, maker spaces, Fab Labs, universities, research institutions, restaurants, businesses and active social movements in neighbourhoods that foster these new values for Barcelona: those of a city that is open, collaborative, democratic, inclusive, productive, circular, innovative and creative." Is Barcelona a sign of things to come?

Local initiatives

There are myriad local initiatives that celebrate togetherness and provide an infrastructure for collaborative action. For example, in the London Borough of Barking and Dagenham there is We Are Everyone, which has created a platform called Every One. Every Day. It is a "a network of 1000s of people living in Barking and Dagenham who are working together on different neighbourhood projects around the borough to make everyday life better for everyone" [61]. It is inspired by a commitment to open source sharing and building creative commons, a new way of thinking for many people and one that challenges the dominant social and economic organisation. Tessy Briton, one of the driving forces behind the project, explains in her blog, *Universal Basic Everything – creating an essential infrastructure for post Covid 19 neighbourhoods*:

> *"Much of our economies in the west have been built on the idea of unique ideas, or inventions, which are then protected and monetised. It's a centuries old way of looking at ideas, but today we also recognise that this method of creating and growing markets around IP protected products has created an unsustainable use of the world's natural resources and generated too much carbon emission and waste."* [62]

Citizen Action

A growing presence in some of Britain's larger cities is the citizens' movement. This is inspired by the community organisations first developed by Saul Alinsky and his colleagues in the USA, and which appeared in the UK in the early 1980s[63]. There were sporadic and largely isolated attempts to build community organisations, but it was not until the advent of Citizens UK in 1996 that a movement began to develop. Crossing party lines and holding politicians to account, there are now nearly 20 citizen action chapters which have achieved some great successes. This is how they describe themselves:

> "Citizens UK is a people power alliance of diverse local communities working together for the common good. Our mission is to develop local leaders, strengthen local organisations which are the lifeblood of their communities and make change. Our member communities are deeply rooted in their local areas. These schools, universities, churches, mosques, synagogues, parent groups, health trusts, charities and unions, are important civic institutions which connect every day to the lives of hundreds of thousands of people"[64].

Locality is another network. This too is a membership organisation with paid organisers that help community groups develop and have clout. They describe themselves as "the national membership network for community organisations" with a simple goal "to help local community organisations be the best that they can be and to create a supportive environment for their work"[65]. Unlike Citizens UK, Locality supports independent community groups.

These examples of collaborative ways of doing things point towards the need for education for cooperation and not just individual advancement.

A new society based on belonging, not alienation

Let us examine where cooperation can lead. We have already mentioned Carson who gives many further case studies of bottom-up community development that explore the possibilities of new technologies and investment in the commons. He concludes[66]:

> *"Tying it All Together ... we've seen a wide variety of municipal initiatives illustrating bits and pieces of a full-blown, commons-based municipal economy. But the different parts are seldom all seen together in the same place. What's needed is to integrate them into a fully fleshed-out ecosystem of information and land commons, cohousing, community gardens, worker and consumer cooperatives, makerspaces and community workshops, coworking spaces, sharing infrastructures to maximize capacity utilization of capital goods and*

reduce the need for ownership, infrastructures for sharing or bartering skills like childcare, local barter currencies and mutual credit, and so forth."

This is a vision of where we might go as traditional social infrastructure and jobs as we know them are destroyed or simply disappear.

Other thinkers are heading in the same direction. Rutger Bregman's *Utopia for Realists and How We Can Get There* elaborates the idea of a universal basic income or dividend (see below). George Monbiot argues in *Out of the Wreckage; A New Politics for an Age of Crisis* that we need to revive our humanity through the politics of belonging. He summarises the past and present:

"We are extraordinary creatures, whose capacity for altruism and reciprocity is unmatched in the animal kingdom. But these remarkable traits have been suppressed by an ideology of extreme individualism and competition. With the help of this ideology, and the story used to project it, alienation and loneliness have become the defining conditions of our time. Far from apprehending them as threats to our wellbeing, we have been induced to see them as aspirations.

"As a result, we find it hard to imagine out of the reaction and helplessness to which we have succumbed. We struggle to recognise, let alone resolve, our common

problems. This has frustrated our potential to do what humans do best: to see the threat to one as a threat to all; and to unite to overcome them.

"To escape from this trap, we first need to perceive it. We need to name the power that has exacerbated our isolation and our collective loss of agency. This power is neoliberalism, the story it tells and the political programmes that arise from it. Our failure to tell a new story with which to replace it has allowed this power to persist and grow.

"By confronting the politics of alienation with a politics of belonging, we rekindle our imagination and discover our power to act."

Like Carson, Monbiot gives a wealth of concrete examples of people building community capital through an emphasis on the commons, a large part of which is the community itself, along with its capacity to organise and develop the rules and systems to sustain itself[67]. Both look to the household and formal co-operatives as key components in this process of building on and extending the commons. And part of this is the 'creation of new sources of shared wealth, based on free and universal access to knowledge'[68]. At the same time, living in cities and towns will revolve around decentralised manufacture with local fab labs like those in Poblenou available for people to make much of what they need. Food production will rely much more on direct relationships between grower and consumer, with large chains and massive supermarkets chasing the shrinking middle.

Co-operatives that work

There are plenty of examples of regeneration that has grown from the bottom upwards. Perhaps the best known is the Mondragon Corporation in Spain[69]. This is composed of 96 co-operatives, collectively employing more than 70,000 people with annual revenues over £10 billion. This has all grown from six people deciding in 1955 that they would operate as a co-operative and invest in their enterprise, rather than siphoning off profits to shareholders. 65 years later the Mondragon co-operatives are flourishing despite the pandemic and financial crises.

In the UK the city of Preston is pioneering a new collaboration between statutory bodies with a commitment to reinvesting in the community[70]. Noticing how public bodies in the area procured goods and services from outside the area, they started to purchase locally and regionally[71]. This has stimulated the local economy. Preston too is promoting workers' co-operatives and helping other councils see how the 'Preston model' might be replicated.

Co-operatives exist throughout the world. With some exceptions like Mondragon, they are usually small enough for people to know each other, and to want to cooperate. Many fail, however, because they get too big and power hierarchies develop, or through poor management, or because they are starved of credit, or because they are too successful[72]. In this last case early owners can sell out to new shareholders, thereby cashing in their investments, and they are in effect converted to capitalist enterprises. Underneath this there is the question of mentality. Frank Lindenfeld and Pamela Wynn write in their blog, *Why Some Worker Co-ops Succeed While Others Fail*:

> *"Co-ops need to develop in their members a sense of solidarity and mutual aid. This may be supplied by ethnic or national identification as among the Basques in Mondragon, or perhaps by identification with the cooperative movement; in any case, co-ops need to have some social basis for solidarity. An organization whose members' core values place individual interests over group interests and has no legitimate source of identity has no foundation on which to build the kind of relationships fundamental to the culture of a cooperative organization."[73]*

Individual interests valued over group interests? Isn't this exactly what our current education system is designed to promote?

The Co-operative Group (now just called the Co-op) has been in existence for over 175 years. Its original objective was to bring people together and to provide services for its members. Although now largely a food retail business with significant extensions into insurance, banking and funeral services, it still is based on members and is ethically oriented in its approach to the 1,000-plus community projects it supports. The Co-op is committed to fairer access to food, mental wellbeing services, education and employment. Many smaller, independent co-ops exist in the UK, mainly around food marketing and distribution. A well-known example is the Suma wholefood co-operative, which has been trading since 1977.

Co-ops appear to go against the dominant trends in society. We are urged to 'put number one first' and this is drummed into everyone through their schooling with its emphasis on individual success. But there are always people for whom collaboration is natural and society matters. The volunteering response to Covid-19 shows this, as do the plethora of self-help organisations such as the Coin Street development (strapline: *Passionate about our neighbourhood*) [74], and the institutions that support self-help such as Grassroots Economic Organising for co-ops and Locality for community organisations [75].

Can co-ops and mutuality lie at the heart of a revolution that will restore meaning to peoples' lives and liberate a collective entrepreneurism at local or regional level? There will always be a need for large businesses to achieve economies of scale, as for example in developing and distributing Covid-19 vaccines or designing and manufacturing electronic components. But as we go into an ever-more uncertain century, let us look to see how to regenerate society at a more local level.

Universal Basic Income (UBI) or Universal Basic Dividend (UBD)

Monbiot and Carson are on the same page as Bregman and Standing in seeing some sort of universal basic income as a key component of this transformation. We see it also as a bedrock that gives people the security to help develop the community-based education infrastructure that we describe in Part Three.

The idea of a universal basic income/dividend (see below on terminology) is that every adult citizen should receive a monthly income irrespective of circumstances. For the worse-off it would replace the myriad benefits systems with their complicated means-tested procedures. At present if someone on benefits takes a temporary job they might have to pay up to 80 or 90% in marginal tax as they lose part or all of their benefits. A UBD would allow people to take on temporary or part-time work, or risk a start-up knowing that their basic income is secure – it is a foundation for investment, not a welfare net. The present benefits system is hideously complex and very expensive to run. It penalises people who want to take a risk and try something out, and it also taxes, rather than encourages, new jobs.

A UBD will encourage entrepreneurism and small start-ups. Where it has been tried in countries as diverse as India, Kenya, Denmark or Canada it has created wealth rather than absorbing it. It is correlated with more money in the household, less spent on alcohol and drugs, with women's emancipation, a greater sense of purpose and especially of agency. Unlike the post-2008 quantitative easing which led to the rich accumulating more assets, a UBD is more likely to be spent, with money kept circulating in the places where people live. It helps to challenge feelings of helplessness and cultures of blame that are being promoted so uncritically. If people do not have to work for such long hours and often in dead-end jobs, they will have more time for family, friendships and fun. They will have time to pursue their interests and acquire new knowledge and develop new skills. They will be able to engage more in community activities that could be anything from sports, playing an instrument or teaching kids how to code. Every aspect of life could be enormously enriched.

Our big-picture analysis so far predicts a world in which business-as-usual will lead to a looming financial crisis with hugely disruptive social effects. Although not a panacea, these effects can be challenged by a UBD.

This concept has a pedigree that goes back over 500 years. It was proposed in Thomas More's *Utopia*, by More's close friend and fellow humanist, Johannes Ludovicus Vives (1492-1540) and by 19th century utopian socialists such as Charlier and Mill. It has had support from such diverse people as Thomas Spence (18th century land reformer) Thomas Paine (author of *Common Sense* and *Rights of Man*) to that effective but unscrupulous politician Richard Nixon. Bismark was influenced by this thinking, as were Clifford Douglas and James Meade[76]. Guy Standing has been arguing the case for over thirty years – he was one of the founding members of the Basic Income Earth Network (BIEN) that has done so much to develop the idea and document its successes[77]. Calls for a UBD are popping up everywhere; many would say that its time has come.

Should we call it Universal Basic Income (UBI) or Universal Basic Dividend (UBD)?

Language is important. Some people object to the term 'Income' as it implies that A (the state) is paying B (the recipient) a regular sum of money. This leads others to ask, "What has B done to deserve it?" "Why should A cough up to support B?" There are unspoken assumptions that hard-working families pay into A so that the Bs of this world can sit around in idleness and exploit their overgenerous compatriots.

Another way of thinking is that every population is endowed with the wealth of the commons as part of its birth-right. The commons include the land, water, air, ecosystem as well as the infrastructure that has been created over the generations – the legal and financial systems, the hospitals and schools, the airports, roads and train tracks. The networks that exist, whether they be trade unions, professional associations or informal community links, can all be seen as part of the commons. Despite current laws that allow people to say, "Hands off! This is mine!" we would argue that nature and previous generations have endowed this to everyone. This investment has produced a dividend, so let this be translated into cash and shared equally – hence the term Universal Basic Dividend or UBD. We believe that UBD is the better term as it forces us to rethink the 'ownership' of wealth and to restore the status of the commons.

Categories of dividend might include a digital dividend (a return for supplying our data to the tech giants) or a citizen's wealth fund (an example is the Alaska Permanent Fund, fed by revenue from exploiting Earth's mineral resources). Or, as Eric Lonergan and Mark Blyth argue in *Angrynomics*, the dividend could be accumulated by government – now able to borrow at negative real interest rates – that could buy up shares and hold them, especially if there is another financial downturn[78]. A carbon dividend is another, related to tackling climate change without punishing the essential use of some fossil fuels[79]. These ideas have a variety of political origins and subtexts, but the direction is clear.

It's all about a share in capital gains, and a share of the economic rents earned by an asset.

How to pay for UBD and taxing unearned income

How will UBD be paid for? Some ideas were included above. Simplifying or replacing state benefits could create immediate savings, provided it is not introduced as chaotically as Universal Credit was in 2013[80]. It can also be part-funded by taxation on unearned income as well as by sharing dividends.

Unearned income is actually a simple concept. If you get richer in your sleep via increased asset values and can earn an economic rent – a surplus above the cost of provision – as part of the fee you charge others to access the asset, then that is unearned income. The present tax system is both immensely complicated and suits only the very rich. Those paying income tax often resent it being given away by the state in benefits and companies dislike having a tax on jobs. But much of the £94 billion hidden subsidies currently given to big business could be redirected towards UBD. Most people today, for example, would support taxing the use of non-renewables such as fossil fuels if there was a compensating carbon dividend.

At a more radical level there could be levies on private ownership or 'enclosure' of the commons, in a land value tax or a pollution tax. After all, the land was not created by human agency; it was privatised and acquired and then rented out. Would a land value tax be acceptable? How about a tax on intellectual property? Many would support taxing intellectual property that is deliberately withheld from use, such as patents for super-efficient motors (held by oil and gas industries) or cheap drugs (held by pharmaceutical companies).

The Amazons, Googles and Facebooks of today make massive profits from selling our data – another form of commons. They use information from our baby photos, shopping habits, holiday destinations, locations, likes and dislikes – indeed just about everything. This information is sold to third parties who use it in targeted advertising. Revelations of Cambridge Analytica's ventures into political advertising are just the tip of the iceberg. Why should the public not benefit from this through taxing enclosure of the digital commons through data harvesting? We give them the data for free. Many platform companies such as Uber appear to avoid paying tax altogether; others like Starbucks move their costs and profits around so that their liability in any one country can be zero. A more rigorous and properly funded tax inspectorate could do wonders for government income.

At present government revenue comes mainly from VAT, corporation tax and PAYE. We must move towards a different tax system that is based more on taxing unearned income. In a future where jobs are decreasing and precarious work becomes the norm, taxes on earned income make less and less sense, at least for the majority of people. Equally, taxes on consumption like VAT will make less sense as more stuff is provided by our own means using repairable or reusable machines, open access digital tools for localised production, renewable energy, vertical farming and so on. A tax on raw materials is preferable in a world that we now recognise as being finite. So is taxing financial transactions (sometimes called a Tobin tax) where transactions occur in microseconds as high-frequency trading algorithms control buying and selling of shares, to no public advantage. This will help manufacturing and related industries, as more financial transactions would be for real, longer-term investments rather than short-term gambling on share prices or so-called financial instruments.

There could be levies on windfalls made when publicly funded infrastructure changes increase the value of property. Examples of this would include what happens to house prices when a new tube station or HS2 appears nearby (well, not *too* near!). When planning permission is granted for a greenfield site the value of the land might increase by up to 1,500%[81].

A Universal Basic Dividend can be seen as a reinvestment in the commons. It would be a recognition that wealth shared can be used to create more wealth by unlocking the creative and entrepreneurial potential of communities – something that is being tried and proved around the world[82].

Creating money to help everyone

Although this could be a book in itself, we need to remember that any country that owns its currency and has stability is not limited in its ability to create money. The question 'How do we pay for it?' might be absurd.

Economist Stephanie Kelton explains this with great clarity[83]. The experiment of so-called quantitative easing showed that money can be created by central banks to acquire troubled bank assets without there being automatic, rampant inflation. It was a pity that this approach was used in response to banks over-creating credit. A quantitative easing for the people is possible, decreasing debt and releasing additional spending, or creating the infrastructure we need today, including the transformation of education. Contrary to received wisdom, there are two 'magic money trees' and one of them is ours, via the government.

Drivers of change and the importance of systems

Across the world millions of people are rattling the bars of the cage. Climate change *is* frightening, yet more and more young people are demanding something better from politicians and the captains of industry. The success of Greta Thunberg's book, *No One is Too Small to Make a Difference*, and the crowds she draws among young people testify to a message that is being heard by many, if not heeded by those in power.

Nobel Peace Prize Laureate Malala Yousafzai is another visible, young woman challenging the assumptions of a white, privileged, patriarchal establishment. She campaigns for universal education for girls. Biden chose to have Amanda Gorman, a young, black, female poet, to read at his inauguration, and a woman of colour as his vice-president. These are minor changes in a society that has deep racist and sexist roots, but they are in the right direction.

The #MeToo movement is prompting people, in particular men, to question behaviours, unconscious assumptions and values. Women will shape a different future, possibly more than in any other era. Many people have observed the countries with the highest Covid-19 death rates have leaders such as Trump, Johnson and Bolsonaro, whereas female-led countries seem to have fared better. The Guardian also reported academic research in August 2020 that "Female-led countries handled coronavirus better" [84]. The Financial Times asked if this is because female leaders have been better than men at rallying their voters to combat the pandemic? [85]

The Black Lives Matter movement is shaking up the way many white people think. Significantly, it is not a centralised organisation with a trademarked name or logo. It is a spontaneous, broad mobilisation of people who reject police violence towards black people and want policies that are anti-racist.

Will radical localism with its commitment to collaboration, the environmental movements, #MeToo and #BlackLivesMatter prove to be the harbingers of a new humanity? Or will localism remain marginal or short-lived, like the Occupy movement, because it does not tackle the hierarchy of power? This trait comes from a belief in networks as a way to bypass entrenched power structures, to be politics-lite, while systems science[86] insists it is the *relationship* between network and hierarchy that shapes effective systems – they are not opposed, but complementary opposites.

An analogy is the blood flow in animals and in humans: the individual cells are nourished by the capillaries but the organism as a whole requires the service of arteries, heart and veins as well. The former, the distributed network, cannot exist except in relationship to the efficient volume flow of the major channels. What needs to change is the emphasis in how we see systems. To be efficient is to be *in service to the distributed* in search of effective enduring and creative evolutionary systems, not the other way around.

A POINT OF TRANSITION

A current joke is that the factory of the future will have only two employees, a man and a dog. The dog is there to make sure that no human gets in to mess up the robots. And the man? Well to feed the dog of course!

As well as automation and artificial intelligence replacing many traditional jobs, there is a trend towards collaborative or social production, with software being almost free and the cost of hardware such as sensors, actuators, 3D printing and other manufacturing technologies falling the whole time. People will start to produce things for themselves, probably working in small groups, as the cost of tools and access to resources continues to fall. This will give space for people to develop their passions. They will not be dependent on institutions or teachers. They will find out and go for what is necessary for them. No longer will they ask, "Who am I? Where do I fit in?" They will go anywhere, any time and do what they do for the joy of living.

In any era of transition there will always be disruption and diversity as things break up. We can see this coming to education as people realise that schools and universities are a huge confidence trick for many people. A degree is no longer a passport to a job. It is more like having permission to buy a lottery ticket to look for a job. But if you go to a prestigious university and make the 'right' contacts, *this* might be the passport to a career. This is what the elites and aspirational middle classes hang on to, and *everyone* is encouraged to believe that this is the thing to strive for. But it is just not available for the many.

In general, schools and universities are producing young people who are conformist rather than creative, anxious rather than confident, fragile rather than resilient, indebted and ill-prepared for modern life. With the inter-related phenomena of economic uncertainty, climate change, the breakdown of social cohesion and the massive changes being brought about by new technologies, few people doubt that we are in a state of disruption which will lead to diversity. It looks now as though the constant raising of schooling's effective leaving age and rapid expansions of provision of higher education were more successful in covering up a lack of jobs than a serious investment in the futures of young people in a way that empowers them to respond creatively to this disruption and diversity.

We are heading for a perfect storm of financial instability, unattainable housing, fewer jobs, fewer public services and a deep unease as shown by the rise of populist demagogues. We would like to see education help people to overcome their anxieties. Let people do exams as and when they want to, but not around a compulsory 'knowledge' curriculum and certainly not in age-determined batches. Once people are freed up from the tyranny of exams and encouraged to pursue learning, there will be no more need for the gatekeepers who tell students if they have passed well enough to go onto the next stage. Indeed, the whole system of qualifications could usefully be taken right out of from learning institutions.

As we have noted earlier, there are many critiques of existing educational systems (in reality, schooling systems) – see for example people like Gert Biesta, Henry Giroux, Danny Dorling and Stephen Ball. There is also a growing movement of people who are revisioning education. Keri Facer is one such person who leads a research programme that is creating new relationships between communities and universities[87].

We want to go one step further. Can we imagine a society in which compulsory schools actually disappear, at least from the age of 14 onwards, and in its place an educational system that encourages passions for learning, justice and beauty, happiness, fun and social responsibility and the skills to face the challenges of the 21st century with creativity and hope?

> *"I've noticed a fascinating phenomenon in my thirty years of teaching: schools and schooling are increasingly irrelevant to the great enterprises of the planet. No one believes anymore that scientists are trained in science classes or politicians in civics classes or poets in English classes. The truth is that schools don't really teach anything except how to obey orders."*
>
> *John Taylor Gatto*

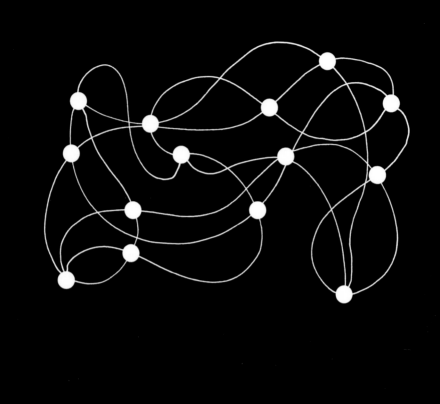

PART THREE: A WAY FORWARD – RETURNING EDUCATION TO THE LEARNERS

INTRODUCTION

A parallel educational system *can* emerge from the pandemic. With the right support, every learner can be self-motivated and keen to learn. Our nature as humans is to explore, question and achieve, to play and have fun. People are driven by both self-interest and sense of responsibility to others. Yet the current system frustrates this. It will be different if we abandon the current emphasis on knowledge, which is debilitating and counter-productive. Exams do not give a satisfactory picture of a student's skills and general aptitudes and are a waste of time and money. Teachers at all levels are seriously demotivated by teaching to the test, which is leading to the crisis in education.

At the same time we know that many parents see good grades in exams as something their children should aspire to. In Part Three we look at how to square this circle. This demands a new paradigm in how we think about education, and the processes of making it happen.

How can we return education to learners in a way that becomes education for agency, fun and fulfilment?

COMMUNITY LEARNING EXCHANGES

We can create networks of Community Learning Exchanges (CLE). The title tells it all. They are based in the community and responsive to local needs. The focus is on self-directed learning without compulsory curricula. And built into the concept is the idea that everyone can be both a learner and a teacher.

The need for a physical centre

Much self-directed learning already happens. A lot of people learn by watching YouTube videos – everything from learning a guitar solo to replacing a lawnmower blade to defeating the baddie in a computer game. Learners follow courses and follow the blogs of people that interest them. A one-stop CLE is a portal for taught courses such as the Khan Academy (earlier strapline *"You can learn anything. For free. For everyone. Forever."*)[88], or more local initiatives such as SynAthina in Athens. Anyone can use the exchange to explore what is available and join it, or just start a group themselves. No one is coerced into following any course; the learners choose freely.

We also need local CLEs that people can relate to physically, a friendly, public building with attractive open spaces. It has a high-quality café as well as rooms and facilities for public use. The café might be linked to programmes for training chefs and others interested in catering and hospitality, with links to local food producers, both traditional farmers and urban horticulturalists.

The CLE includes well-resourced maker labs, performance and practice areas, studios, meeting spaces and a library containing books and other resources. It is a place for people to meet, sit around, work individually or in groups, and have fun. It is home to a range of services, a real community hub. In a small town there would be just one CLE, in larger towns or cities there would be a network of them. The CLE is a network of learning opportunities.

The CLE creates learning opportunities for local people, underpinned by the elected local authority with statutory responsibility to find out what people of all ages want, and to encourage others (businesses and community groups as well as individuals) to see that the resources are there. The authority becomes more enabling platform than provider.

Three roles for learning exchange staff

The CLE has open access for anyone aged 14 or older. It provides learning **mentors** or life coaches to help learners decide what they want to do and the routes for getting there. Professional **resources managers** help learners identify suitable resources – written word, podcast or video – or **experts** with identifiable skills. Some **experts** will work in businesses or institutions dedicated to research or transmission of skills (as in apprenticeships). Let us examine these in more detail.

Mentors

The mentors or coaches meet their learners regularly. Sensitive listeners and creative thinkers, they steer the learner into acquiring necessary skills for them to develop their chosen projects.

Examples of mentors' advice

A group wanting to grow vegetables for sale in a local market needs to learn horticulture, marketing and food safety. They would also need numeracy and a wide range of communication skills. They learn these in the pursuit of their own project, not because some remote curriculum authority demands it.

Another group developing an improved anaerobic digester needs maths and science to underpin their research, anything from the chemistry of fermentation to fluid dynamics to optimise flows in pipes.

Mentors help learners to find fruitful ways to pursue their aims. All will need numeracy, communication and critical thinking.

Mentors encourage students to pursue their passions *and* to stretch themselves beyond their immediate zones of comfort, to challenge them with new ideas. Mentors are inspirational and reactive as self-directed learning is new for many people. They can enthuse learners towards areas that they had never heard of let alone thought about. Mentoring demands the traditional skills of asking questions to open up possibilities, more than supervising knowledge acquisition.

With the help of their mentors, everyone can find something they want to do. Basic skills of communication, literacy, numeracy, economic and media awareness, creativity and critical thinking will be learned largely in school up to the age of 14. CLE mentors see if catch-up is needed and advise accordingly. Many ex-teachers find fulfilment in mentoring as it is more rewarding than teaching large groups of children topics that they are not necessarily interested in.

Mentors pay attention to learners' physical and psychological wellbeing and are concerned with safeguarding generally. They identify and support those with special educational needs (especially younger learners), referring them to a specialist as necessary. There are very few young learners (currently described as NEETs) as they go for something of their own choosing and approach it with enthusiasm.

Such mentoring is available throughout life. Mentors help young learners who are not yet sure of their direction of travel as much as someone pursuing a vocational course in coding, accountancy or law. Mentors support people at a change in life, such as when they retire or are seeking new work, or have to reorient everything as they become parents or need to look after a relative.

Mentors are recruited from existing teachers, coaches, psychologists or social workers, and from business and industry – see section on recruitment below. These latter help with communication skills, time planning, discussion of possible job opportunities and give guidance on project management, as well as personal support. As learning is intrinsically a social activity, mentors help people find learning buddies so that they can explore things together.

Since each curriculum is unique to each learner and chosen by them in conjunction with their mentor, learners could choose to study at home, in the CLE, a work environment or indeed anywhere.

The mentors have almost a coaching function and are at the heart of the CLE.

Resources managers

Resource managers deploy personal, social and organisational skills to help learners find the right resource. Teams of resources managers build up local contacts with libraries, museums, businesses and voluntary and statutory bodies in the area.

Examples of Resources Managers' work

They put on traditional classes for groups of learners who have similar interests and aspirations. They arrange a week in the country for a group that wanted outdoor learning, or a visit to a gallery or county court.

They help place someone in a suitable work experience environment.

They look after CLE physical spaces with rooms for performances, laboratories for investigations, design studios, maker labs for building prototypes or one-off products, facilities for sports.

Resource managers maintain a database of all groups, businesses and information resources in their area. They collaborate at a regional level and feed into national information banks.

Experts

A third role is for experts. These too are drawn partially from the ranks of existing teachers and lecturers as well as industry and commerce. If a group of learners wants to study English literature for example, put on a play or learn to speak French, resources managers support this by finding a suitable specialist or expert. Experts also organise vocational instruction opportunities and work placements for learners to develop specific skills. These might be anything from plumbing or wiring to mechanical engineering, coding, games design or community organising. Someone embarking on a vocational course in a trade such as bricklaying and plastering, or white-collar profession such as accountancy, law or architecture, needs expert instruction. Such instruction is not the same as mentoring, which is more akin to coaching as the learner progresses through life.

One of the roles of the mentors is help their students to get the best out of their experts, and this includes not being bamboozled into thinking that their expert's way is the only way.

RECRUITMENT

How might mentors, resources managers and experts be recruited? Existing teachers will become mentors, resources managers, or experts staying within their area of expertise. But crucially, this will be demand-led and in response to the wishes of the learners. Mentors will also be recruited from coaches, psychologists or social workers.

There will always be a demand for brilliant historians, inspirational mathematics teachers, practising musicians and artists. The inspirational teacher must not be lost – nothing is more inspirational than passion and love of their own specialism. There will be opportunities for them to demonstrate their expertise and passion, such as open evenings or fairs.

But CLE staff will be drawn from a pool of talent far wider than qualified teachers. Every settlement has a huge and largely untapped human capital that could be mobilised through a CLE. This includes retired people and those between jobs. It is not confined to the professional classes. Bringing people together through CLEs enhances respect and social cohesion, especially since it involves teachers and learners of all ages and interests. People with hobbies can be drawn into their local network.

Firms or individuals can sign contracts with funding bodies to second staff as instructors or mentors for so many hours a week or year. The current divisions between education and training, or between the mis-named 'practical' and 'academic' study would dissolve as the barriers between education and work disappear. It manifests a basic truth – that learning occurs everywhere and throughout life. The current structure of the education industry hides this and serves to further frustrate it by limiting free education to children ages 4 to 19.

Part of this reframing is to see every business or workplace as a potential learning resource. At present, individuals and businesses are taxed to pay for schools and colleges. Organised at a national level there is little connection between the taxpayers in any town or city and the educational provision there. Could the concept of apprenticeships be expanded so that there are far more opportunities for learners to work in conjunction with a local company and for this to be paid for via tax exemptions? Could ex-teachers join the staff of companies to expand and manage their educational offer?

Each team of resource managers will have a business development strand to their work. Companies or statutory bodies will collaborate to ensure there is an adequate supply of trained personnel (e.g. nuclear engineers, bricklayers, radiologists) and no doubt professional institutions will continue to provide accreditation for certain occupations. There will still be a role for national or regional government to look at labour supply in certain industries, but a regional network of CLEs will be far better attuned to local needs and more capable of responding quickly.

THE FUTURE OF JOBS IN EDUCATION

At present most teachers and lecturers have jobs. In schools these are usually permanent, whereas in higher and further education the trend is towards zero-hours or short-term employment.

As many traditional jobs disappear and people can survive on a universal basic dividend, there will be a huge pool of talented people with diverse skills, who can find meaning in life through contributing their expertise to learning through local or digital learning exchanges. Over time this will have a profound effect on the existing teaching professions. The present system of a compulsory curriculum determined by central government, standardised assessment and competition between schools based on league tables, leaves many secondary school teachers feeling de-professionalised. They are more akin to delivery managers in the middle ranks of schooling institutions. This is far removed from the inspiration or idealism that brought them into the teaching professions in the first place. In any case, the growth of artificial intelligence and remote learning will also hollow out the jobs of many in the traditional teaching professions.

There will still be large companies like Pearson Education running a transnational examination business. There will still be some traditional schools, colleges and universities for those who seek a prescribed system. As learning networks develop and grow there will still be many jobs for teachers or their successors as mentors, resource managers and experts, and many small, localised or specialist enterprises in and around CLEs. But old career paths of being a classroom teacher, head of department, assistant head and so on will be severely limited. Teaching will become a much more flexible career and probably there will be fewer who take it on for life. It will be the same in many of the established professions. This is a great opportunity for people to share what they have to offer with a far wider range of people as the CLEs and networks attract people of all classes and ages, and their sense of self-worth is not dependant on exams passed in earlier life.

PEDAGOGY – PROJECT-BASED LEARNING

At the heart of this reform is a migration from knowledge-based towards project-based learning. This is based on a simple premise. The learner, in conjunction with their mentor and possibly their employer, decides to embark on a learning journey that is rooted in a real-life interest. They decide on the broad aim of the project. It will be anything from creating an app, recording an album, designing and making a rack for drying linocuts, developing optimal conditions for growing lettuce, performing as a comic or building a website. It could be organising a 5-a-side football tournament for local children or running a health education campaign around substance abuse. It could be to develop a business plan around a new app or to plan a low-price food stall for a festival.

It might be totally 'impractical' (a better word than 'academic'), such as a scientific investigation of a phenomenon that the learner finds interesting or investigating whether King Richard lll has an undeserved reputation thanks to his portrayal by Shakespeare. Or it might be totally 'practical' such as designing and building a bicycle trailer, improving Grandma's garden or cooking for Eid. The variety of project aims is limitless. They can be tightly focused, leading to a specific conclusion (testing a scientific hypothesis), or open-ended in scope (improving one's football skills). Even then, tightly focused projects will always open up questions, on reflection, and one role of mentors is to encourage this.

In a project the learner (with support from their mentor as needed) plans and executes research, looks at project costs and how they might be met, makes a time plan and considers alternative routes to meeting the aim. They develop a more precise set of objectives or even criteria for success. They will reflect on progress and modify their plans accordingly, often doing further research. This research could be a primary investigation or based on information from others. In the course of a project the student might have some very specific tasks such as gaining an understanding of the concept of molecular weight (perhaps via a Khan Academy course on chemistry) or learning how to solve equations. Over time the learners move towards some realisation of their project brief, some activity or physical product to help fulfil their aim. It is a constant cycle of action, investigation and reflection.

Projects can be individual enterprises. But there are many more group projects and ones that are related to meeting local needs. This recognises that learning is also a contextualised, social activity. One of the joys of learning through projects is that it lends itself naturally to collaborative learning. It is an approach to learning has been around for a long time – at least from the time of Plato's Academy in Athens[89]. It was articulated by John Dewey[90] in the early 20th century and has been the basis of much primary years' education. Sometimes it is called 'learning by doing'. It is a movement that is growing across the world[91].

It is seen in the current school curriculum in subjects such as design and technology, in the International Baccalaureate Diploma's extended essay, and in the UK exam boards' Extended Project Qualifications, but it is not widespread. There is growing research evidence that, as learners articulate the purpose of what they are doing, they are more motivated and learn better. Projects have a value in real life far greater than passing an exam.

At the end of the project the learners sometimes give a presentation to their peers (whoever they might be) and maybe to their mentors and other experts whom they have recruited along the line. Most importantly, mentors encourage learners to record what they have achieved and what they have learned – important if applying for a job but useful also for encouraging critical reflection on their experience.

As learners progress through life they build up a portfolio of their projects through which they can communicate their thoughts, ideas, successes and failures and what they have learned, as well as reflections on their learning process. These are written, drawn, spoken, performed and filmed using all manner of communications technologies. This provides far better evidence of a person's capabilities and potential than a score in the widely discredited system of public exams.

LEARNER PROGRESSION, ASSESSMENT AND ACCREDITATION

This raises questions of accreditation. At school, the pervasive, hugely expensive and largely uninformative enterprise of public examinations with their associated course books will change beyond all recognition if it does not actually wither away. Most schools as exam factories will gradually cease to exist as the alternatives are seen to be more attractive, more locally relevant and more dedicated towards learning. For those who want them, universities will still offer traditional courses and degrees at bachelors, masters and doctoral level, and be centres of excellence in research. But following one of these pre-designed courses will become the exception. Many new, part-time and short courses are already emerging in response to Covid restrictions. As AI develops, vocational and professional institutions will revise what bundles of skills and knowledge they require and what evidence they need to be certain that an individual had these skills. No doubt they would still set exams relevant to their trades and professions. But potential employers will have also a far richer source of information in a project portfolio as to what a potential applicant can offer, especially in the soft skills of teamwork and communication, the skills in systems thinking and, above all, resilience.

MEANINGFUL ASSESSMENT

People paid to work in an effective learning system should be able to show that there are giving value for money, and that 'their' learners are progressing. Or should they? The huge contradiction of having operational definitions of progress is that the funders demand that things are getting better year-on-year, or rather, can be *seen* to be getting better. This leads to a defined curriculum, tests, teaching to the tests and all the counter-educational experiences that result.

Here is an alternative that would work if people have not lost sight of reality through building themselves up or criticising others on social media. Why not ask the learners to evaluate their learning on a cyclical basis, using criteria that they themselves think are important? This has some immediate advantages.

- The learners give feedback that the educators can use for improving their offer

- It helps to create respect and collaboration between teachers and learners

- It embodies a dialogical approach to teaching and learning

- It overcomes the dangers of the provider knowing what is good for the learners and imposing it; this is especially important in cross-cultural education

- It is based in the real-life needs of the learners

- It provides a point of reference for the learners to reflect on their learning and what they can do to embed it

- The way that the criteria changed over time for any cohort would itself give insights as to what was important.

Mentors working in a CLE could build a model of user-led evaluation and assessment. It could demonstrate year on year how their activities were developing in a way that would impress their funders as well as providing genuinely useful feedback for planning. Above all it would involve the learners in self-assessment. They would, with the help of their mentors and peers, reflect critically on their progress and be able to articulate what they had achieved. This is a tried and tested part of current education in art, design and technology and in practical science.

LIFELONG LEARNING IN THE COMMUNITY BASED ON NEW PRINCIPLES

Open to everyone

A central feature of a CLE is that it is available to people of all ages. Many people register both as teachers and learners. There are seldom age restrictions in learning groups in which everyone is expected to behave like adults. Lifelong learning has been discussed forever but it is not promoted, because governments and the educational establishments are locked into a nationally controlled, provider model of education. CLEs will certainly challenge this.

This radical model provides an alternative framework for many schools and colleges, vocational training institutions, community development programmes, business support and regional development agencies, careers advice, public libraries, maker labs and much of what is currently done in institutions of higher education. It returns learning to the learner. Well-resourced CLEs open up real possibilities of life-long learning. They locate learning in the heart of a community whilst also providing support for DIY and remote learning. It is an authentic, imaginative approach to education in which learners move towards freedom and autonomy and take *ownership* of learning. This is so unlike the current provider-led model that actually inhibits learners' taking responsibility for their learning. The underlying educational principles are spelt out in Appendix A.

Localism and why a compulsory national curriculum cannot empower learners

We are calling for a new localism in education and the creation of learning communities at a local level. Education and community development can go hand in hand, responsive to local needs and the wishes of learners. A national curriculum was well intended (we hope) as a means of giving every child the same access to knowledge, the same rights to learn. But it does not work; inequalities still exist, too many children are bored or suffer from anxiety and stress as they fear failure. Many teachers at all levels are fed up and leaving the profession. There is a profound disconnect that leaves people feeling powerless with no sense of purpose or agency. This radical reframing of the way we think about learning, and the new CLE infrastructure, will be at the heart of learner empowerment.

Moving towards a democratic and open approach to learning has huge benefits to individuals and society as a whole. Throughout history the political, economic and cultural establishments resisted such change, maintaining that unleashing such forces of innovation and self-help would be dangerously disruptive. Dangerous for whom? Creative disruption is exactly what is needed. It involves rediscovering the roots of real education. And it helps people address the challenges of the 21st century in a positive, resilient and exciting way.

Making the most of remote learning

In many ways the computer revolution has yet to reach schools and colleges. Yes, there are computers, whiteboards and multimedia workshops in every educational establishment. Most students have access to a computer, tablet and phone and know how to use them. Students are encouraged to access materials online, and virtual learning environments are flourishing. But this is still within the factory model of education with the people in charge remaining in charge, deciding what should be learned and how it should be learned, operating a transmission model of learning and trying to make it more efficient. Few institutions encourage mutual learning groups around a common interest and use this as the prime resource of their education. The flipped learning model whereby content is acquired remotely, and classes used for digesting and making sense of it, is still not the norm.

Today almost anything can be looked up. What is needed is the ability to look at information critically and be able to examine one's own biases, recognising the increasing difficulty of getting reliable information or arguable material, when algorithms drive for attention not veracity. Nonetheless, education institutions have hardly started to explore the unlimited online opportunities coming through, not least because they are in thrall to meaningless targets and are stuck in a transmission model. The pandemic is encouraging new thinking. Most people under 40 carry the world with them on their phones, although this cornucopia is not always recognised and phones can provide a distraction from reality. Artificial intelligence will generate all sorts of possibilities including each learner having their personalised AI learning assistant.

How to get from A to B

The hardest thing when proposing disruptive change is to identify a roadmap, a mechanism for getting from A to B. How can we move from a centralised state system of education with compulsory curricula, a DHL model of delivery of knowledge and big business running standardised testing, towards the sort of liberating education we describe above?

There is no blueprint for such a transition; it is something that will develop organically in the light of feedback from a wide spread of stakeholders – learners old and young, teachers and educational administrators, and people from schools, colleges, universities, businesses, community groups, libraries and elected authorities – indeed anyone with a stake in learning. It might start in a limited way in any town with, for example, the establishment of a maker lab and café with ultrafast Wi-Fi in a public space, a commitment by those in adult education and some businesses to work together, support for open access software to encourage mutuality and exchanges, and minimal staffing (possibly appointed by the current educational authority) to underpin its development. Governance issues will vary from place to place. No blueprint then, but we can identify some events that will move society in the right direction.

We need a new Great Debate on the purpose of schools, colleges and universities, based on a commitment to widening participation. Such discussion will open the doors for change but does not have the power to take people through. Energy for change will come from widespread dissatisfaction and disruption. This energy exists already among many students and their parents. They want to be happy and do something meaningful and interesting but are frightened of standing out against the culture of conformity. Fear of uncertainty is exacerbated during a crisis and risk-taking diminishes – if anything, people resile in old attitudes and want more traditional education.

Yet we are at a moment in history with a perfect storm of looming environmental collapse, rapid social change and financial chaos. This is why we need some form of UBD – to make it wise to take risks and try something out.

As more parents see the flaws of what is offered in the mainstream and some even opt for home education, or parents are punished for having children out of school, and more students say that enough is enough and become more disruptive, more teachers will remember why they entered the profession want to do something different. The accelerating breakdown in morale among teachers is an inevitable consequence of a system that is both fundamentally flawed and dishonest. Yet this collapse of confidence and rediscovery of the purpose of education both offer the possibility of change.

A few local authorities, academy chains or other groups of schools might establish community learning exchanges of the sort described above, perhaps with business support. It will be a bold experiment and would need to be done in conjunction with local vocational colleges, businesses and universities. It will be available for 14-year-olds and upwards. In time there will need to be enabling legislation and new financial arrangements. The costs need not be prohibitive as much of the physical infrastructure is already there. We come back to finance issues below.

Thus a CLE might develop in any town or small city, or in part of a larger conurbation alongside the existing infrastructure of schools, colleges and higher education. There remains a need for a physical hub based on a café and to include leisure facilities, workshops and studio spaces. As engagement expands it can develop into a network of institutions, many of which will remain independently run and financed. As more groups and businesses come in, and opportunities for teachers and learners expand, there will be growing flexibility in who can offer what. Throughout life, people will have the opportunity both to learn and to teach.

The organisational infrastructure to underpin this will be an enabling platform more than a provider. It would *not* be a vehicle for delivering programmes created at the top and delivered downwards. Many core staff will come from existing schools, preferring to be based in a physical or virtual learning exchange as a mentor or resources manager, or as an expert instructor. As the money for adult education has been so cut over the decades and since the CLE will be available to people of all ages, there might need to be transitional arrangements for charging adults; but then this happens in adult education already. What would be new is that adults and teenagers would be in the same groupings to their mutual benefit.

Flexibility

As these approaches are fundamentally more successful that the existing model, there will be a positive effect on literacy, communication skills and numeracy. Young people will be more determined, hopeful, resilient, more inclined to collaborate and take responsibility for their own lives. They will be happier. More people will gravitate towards CLEs as an alternative to schools. For older people it will be a whole new opportunity. Learners will mix and match with some formal exam-based learning and some DIY activities via the CLE. Bit by bit, some schools will be transformed into democratic learning networks with a different ethos and purpose. There will always be some classical schools and universities; our class structure will ensure that. There will always be parents who want to give their children a leg up into a 'higher' class and the chance to mix with the 'right' people. But the opportunities for the 93% who currently have to undergo compulsory schooling will have a genuine alternative. So too will the 7% whose parents often scrimp and save to buy advantage for their children through sending them through the private schooling system. Some state and privately funded institutions will offer something similar to the current regime of GCSEs, A levels and degrees. The expanding, parallel system offers choice and the chance of self-directed learning, and a recovery of agency among learners.

THE PAINS OF TRANSITION

Here we address a number of issues that cause concern, and how problems might be overcome.

Number of Jobs

Will there be more or fewer jobs in education? The nature of jobs is already changing and the CLE model will allow people to vary their roles between teaching and learning throughout life. There will be fewer full-time teachers with a life-long commitment to this as a career. It will be easier for people to slip in and out of teaching, mixing and matching this with other occupations. No one can tell for certain if there would be a net gain or loss in educational employment, not least because the concept of 'employment' will change with UBD. Salaried teachers who remain on the books will certainly be part of a far healthier and more motivated workforce with all the savings that that would entail. There will be wider use of enthusiastic but 'unqualified' learning experts or coaches, supported by basic training in different teaching skills.

A more pluralistic system will emerge, one driven by many converging trends. The huge possibilities of online learning and self-directed study supported by the development of CLEs as described above will disrupt the factory model of the school and university. Teachers as gatekeepers or learning controllers will go the same way as sailmakers, bespoke tailors or milliners, all valued and needed in small numbers in society. But teachers will no longer be part of a big, pervasive, vertically integrated business with a captive market.

More widely, education and training available throughout life and facilitated by CLEs, and underpinned by UBD, will free a huge entrepreneurial boom. In this way jobs will be created.

Safeguarding

Safeguarding is a real issue for people at every age. We do not pretend to have all the answers, but these seem salient issues for a CLE developing its safeguarding practices.

Every revolution is open to people abusing the new systems. In formal education the present system fails many pupils and their teachers. Not every educational institution is necessarily a safe space from sexual harassment or bullying by peers, neglect or inappropriate attention from staff. Failing exams or being told one is underperforming can damage a young learner's confidence for life. Teachers and students can have their confidence and reputations ruined by unfair allegations.

The teaching professions have made massive strides in developing cultures of care and respect within their institutions but there is still an overriding acceptance of coercion to achieve conformity. In our proposed non-hierarchical and participatory scenario, careful consideration will be given to protecting learners and their educators including protection from personal abuse or charlatans.

Could CLE participants build up an online reputation that new teachers and learners could check out before signing up with someone? Could quality assurance be based in part on a reputational approach similar to the profiling that builds up on TripAdvisor, Airbnb or eBay? Mentors, resources managers and experts could have ratings given to them, as could adult learners. DBS checks or similar will still be needed for any adult working in or via a CLE. But beneath that there would be a presumption of mutual trust.

Will mixing teenagers with adults lead to disaster? Older teenagers encouraged to act in a more adult way can give fair assessments of their teachers and mentors, and vice versa. Remember that the system in existing institutions is far from perfect. The fact that someone qualified as a teacher thirty years ago or was appointed to a university lectureship on the basis of published research does not ensure that they are a good or safe teacher today. Security gates and swipe cards literally makes barriers between schools and colleges and the rest of life and we are proposing that learning is integrated into the life of community for people of all ages. A few unsuitable people will always slip through the net. In CLEs the emphasis will be more on developing systems that promote a community culture in which people look out for and support each other. This is huge challenge but one that will have to be addressed.

Antisocial behaviour

There is no fail-safe system for preventing downright antisocial behaviour. But an education infrastructure that does not divide people at key points in their lives into failures or successes will help: one which is learner-led and which enhances learners' experience of agency and achievement will serve to address the causes of antisocial activity.

The heart of responsible behaviour is an explicit commitment by everyone to be respectful and look out for each other. Some issues are very personal and not resolvable in a learning environment. But belief in mutual support is a strong foundation for personal development. The other pillar of good practice is the principle that everyone is responsible for their own safety and wellbeing. Real safety does not come from blind or forced adherence to a rulebook. It comes from an awareness of possible dangers and the best ways to ameliorate a dangerous predicament.

Most situations require an agreed code of conduct. In the UK we drive on the left, give priority to traffic already on a roundabout and have speed limits on roads. But it is careful and attentive driving that lies at the heart of road safety. The analogy here is that learners and teachers will understand and share safe and respectful attitudes and behaviours. Every CLE will have a charter of good practice (as many schools do now), expressed in principles rather than rules. This would include a specific contract that all concerned signed up to. If there was a clear breach in acceptable behaviour a learning group or mentor would have to have the ability to exclude someone.

People ask whether this would lead to feral teenagers roaming the streets, uncontained and threatening the law-abiding citizen. There will always need to be juvenile centres or referral units, whatever one chooses to call them. But CLEs will create opportunities in which individuals are trusted, encouraged and supported in pursuing *their* interests; this will actually cut off a lot of crime before it starts. A few people will rebel against anything that is offered. Perhaps rebelling against the current system of schools as exam factories is healthy and the dissatisfaction growing among young people could be a powerful motor for change. But how would the CLE cope with a stroppy or ill-mannered learner, or a person with health issues that makes them difficult to work with?

There is no reason why it should fall to educators to be responsible for this. Could the prime responsibility for keeping law and order revert to parents and child welfare officers in the case of minors, and the police, medical professions and social workers who must be properly resourced? It need not be expected of people whose prime interest is education and sharing knowledge and expertise.

A new social contract

At the heart of this is a new social contract through which, at a local level, the people of a town or part of a larger city collectively take responsibility for education. People engaged in the CLEs network could sign a pledge to this effect. A condition of working with and through a CLE could be to offer as well as receive, both for individuals and for groups. This is an idealistic vision – but why not? We start from the premise that people naturally want to help each other and that everyone has something to offer someone else. This part of our nature was demonstrated in the community response to the Covid crisis. This is a recipe for living in hope and trust, rather than the fear and suspicion that drive much of the current educational system.

GOVERNANCE ISSUES – HOW MIGHT A LOCAL CLE BE MANAGED?

Community learning exchanges will be rooted in their local communities. Governance is hugely complicated and, whatever the structure, the guiding principle must be transparency. Current systems of oversights by boards of unaccountable governors (appointed by whom?), local authorities, academy trusts, Ofsted, religious groups, national government and professional associations all conspire against community involvement. Let learning exchanges see themselves as open-ended facilitating platforms rather than providers of a specified and hence limited range of services. Let each develop its own community-oriented governance structure.

Governance needs to be open to all types of stakeholder and be responsive to local demand. Each CLE will have its charter and social contract to which all participants would sign up. A model set of principles for charters could be enshrined in law, but this should not stand in the way of local priorities. The principles would include openness, transparency and financial accountability, a commitment to quality, responsiveness to local needs, safety and inclusivity. Governing bodies must be accessible to, and shaped, by people of all backgrounds and interests.

Within this will be some mechanism for challenging anyone (but especially businesses, government or faith groups) who tries to assert their own agendas and make everyone else conform. But this need not be a remote, external agency like Ofsted. Far better would be a local forum backed up by the county court. With the right charter and the right social contract, most disputes would be over the fulfilment or non-fulfilment of contracts. To arrive at this, CLEs will be facilitated initially by the local authority in conjunction with existing educational providers but with a commitment to their becoming independent institutions, free of political control, as soon as possible.

How to pay for a community learning exchange

We anticipate that in any community some of the expert teaching would be given free in the same way that experienced people with allotments are willing to show the ropes to newcomers. With a universal basic dividend there will be fresh opportunities for sharing knowledge and expertise; as stated elsewhere, over a period of time most people would be both learners and teachers. Individuals, groups or businesses could be given learning vouchers or tokens that could be exchanged for learning opportunities. People who collected them could recycle them on learning opportunities for themselves. These learning vouchers must be available throughout life, or available in volume for someone who wanted to pursue some expensive vocational training in, say, medicine or engineering. Mentors, resources managers and experts could be on salaries or on piecework contracts in the way that many university academics are today. Many people will have unique life paths that take them in and out of paid employment over the years. Already the current model of being educated, qualified and then a career for life is no longer the norm.

Basic infrastructure costs will be met from taxation. As more young people turn towards learning exchanges and away from current statutory providers, some cash will come from savings in schools and related services. A general improvement in health and wellbeing will generate savings in children's and other social services, as well as health budgets. All these areas have been starved of funds especially since the financial crash of 2008 and successive governments choosing austerity. But all political parties share the rhetoric of needing to invest in education, even if they have little understanding of what education actually is.

It already costs some £8,500 per year to keep a child in secondary school. Some of these funds could be reallocated to the local CLE. It will clearly be expensive initially but there will be massive savings in the long run with less truancy and fewer people with mental health issues, less demand on social workers and the forces of law and order. It is a risk worth taking.

Finally, many funding issues will disappear as we move towards a universal basic dividend, or even a limited initiative such as a citizens' wealth fund that gives £10,000 to each 25-year-old[92]. Although the development of CLEs can start now without UBD, the freedom and stimulation that UBD will bring will transform everyone's possibilities for the future.

Business interest

How will businesses invest in community learning? There has been a long-standing tradition of the state providing free education and training and businesses being able to benefit directly from a qualified workforce – yet there is widespread dissatisfaction within business about the narrow curriculum and lack of skills among school and university leavers.

Professional training is different as law, accountancy and architectural students (for example) have to pay tuition and exam fees prior to qualification. CLEs will not affect this, especially for people training for national or international qualifications. With CLEs responsive to local needs and many SMEs interested in recruiting locally, business will have an interest both in shaping training and using the exchanges for recruitment.

Already many individuals in business give their free time to help others with coaching or advice. A significant regional industry might well wish to invest heavily in training, in the way that engineering companies needed to work with training providers when creating a qualified workforce to build the North Sea wind farms. A local business enhances its public profile by being seen to be an active stakeholder in building links in the community. CLEs will create interesting new opportunities for developing training. Businesses can be encouraged through tax rebates, reducing the apprenticeship levy or through some other mechanism.

RETURNING LEARNING TO THE LEARNERS

A learning network will bring together much of what is best in community development, schools, FE and apprenticeships, and some parts of universities. The latter will become far more flexible, offering non-examined modules and modular degrees that can be built up over the years. University students will have far greater opportunities to mix and match and carve out individual pathways. CLEs will pull together adult education opportunities including libraries and classes, arts and crafts, maker labs, sports clubs and community groups. They might be the basis for public science, festivals of ideas or the arts. They could be a launchpad for innovative businesses, for community health campaigns, for heritage research. They could be support centres for home educators. They would certainly afford the opportunity for likeminded people to come together and develop common projects and above all to enjoy life. The opportunities are endless, and exciting as we move towards wildly different notions of work and jobs, and more time for creative and joy-filled endeavours.

CONCLUSION

There is no good reason why CLEs or rather networks of CLEs should not become the norm for post-14 education, with traditional classes becoming the exception. Since information is freely available on the web and learning groups can be formed so easily, flipped learning will surely become standard practice. Rather than having fearful students who are taught to be led and to conform, we will have a growing body of resilient citizens, more capable of creatively addressing the challenges of the 21st century and who have learned how to learn. UBD can unlock this access to human and physical resources at a time when the whole concept of jobs is changing and we move towards a more human, sharing economy.

This is a radical proposal but there are many green shoots. We have attempted a synthesis of best practice both past and present. It is a democratic proposal that will encourage people to have more agency in their lives and which will encourage collaboration and investment in the local community. In building sharing communities, the local skills and learning exchanges will be real schools for democracy.

> *"Education is not preparation for life; education is life itself."*
>
> *John Dewey*

Appendix A

We need to move from focusing on the *acquisition of knowledge* as expressed in memorising propositions that can be tested in exams, towards *learners' empowerment* in a complex world in ways that build their confidence and resilience.

Part of this is moving away from an emphasis on *solving problems* and towards *appreciation of a problem or predicament and* the *reframing of questions* that need to be addressed. If learners are only given a real-life problem to solve there is always a danger they will use a linear or Enlightenment-based approach to come up with a solution. Sometimes this is a useful way of thinking but too many problems are framed in a simplistic way.

The linear problem-solving approach attempts to find simple cause and effect and to seek a remedy. Through education, learners need to stand back, to look beyond the obvious system boundaries, to look at problematic phenomena in the round and consider how they are manifestations of a complex system. Learners need to identify some of the feedback loops and the possible effects of making some changes. A valuable life skill is to be able to reframe questions in a way that will optimise the workings of the system whilst recognising that knowledge is always limited and partial, and that there is seldom a simple solution to be found.

In part this means moving away from focusing on *skills of analysis* and towards *skills of synthesis*. Learners must try to look at the whole picture. Rather than reducing the area of investigation to its simplest parts, they need to emphasise an understanding of the wider system. The Enlightenment taught us to categorise and abstract, to assume that events take place in a closed system, and to seek cause and effect. The 21st century learner will look for multiple influences across time and space. Many people struggle to understand the British vote to leave the European Union (Brexit) or Donald Trump's popularity in the United States in terms of cause and effect. The shallowness of much comment even in the more intelligent media shows the inadequacy of an Enlightenment model of thinking as peoples' votes are ascribed to greed and complacency, racism, stupidity, or dishonesty.

The current dominant model of *individual learning* is narrow and needs to be more open to *social learning in teams or groups*. Not only is this more effective and at times cheaper to organise, it is also more real and likely to produce deeper understandings. This is not to say that individual learning is not needed: understanding of number bonds, skills in drawing or spelling, the correct use of a tool, how to drive a bus or understanding of shearing forces (for an engineer) are things that have to be acquired and internalised at an individual level. But even then, there are places for this to be done through group activity.

This leads on to the need to move from learning being almost exclusively *competitive* to encouraging *both competition and collaboration*. People are social beings and collaborative learning needs to be the norm, especially as learners tease out the complex workings of systems. The argument that assessment becomes difficult if individual, unseen examinations are scrapped does not matter both because exams mainly test a student's ability to do exams and secondly because they give little indication of motivation, resilience and broad capability.

For all this to happen we need to move away from *teachers being transmitters of predetermined knowledge* and towards *learning through enquiry and projects*. The dichotomy between teachers as experts and learners as ignorant, or teachers being the active thinkers and the learners the passive recipients must be replaced by a commitment to self-directed enquiry and project-based learning.

This in turn requires moving from *curricula being compulsory* and determined by remote experts who know what is good for you and towards individual and group learning journeys in which the *learners take responsibility for their own learning*, both in content and in methods.

Disciplines and subjects – currently the basis of almost every school, college or university timetable – need to be replaced by an emphasis on *meta-learning*[93] in which learners 'become aware of and increasingly in control of habits of perception, inquiry, learning, and growth that they have internalised'. The enduring status of subjects and disciplines more than anything inhibits the development of real learning.

The desired outcome is that learners move from developing *passivity* and compartmentalised knowledge towards their being the *creative agents of history*, able to understand systems and how best to intervene in them to make the world a better place.

Appendix B

We have argued against compulsory curriculum for education. In an ideal world there would be a basic education in which experience is the bedrock. In primary and middle years (up to 14) children will have the opportunity to develop their innate love of play and learning, growing in confidence and skills in communication, understanding complexity and seeing how things connect, as well as in analysis. Learning must be rooted in real life. So let the arts and drama play a central part of discovering this – the lessons of Reggio Emilia and Steiner are fundamentally sound. Let every learner be comfortable with creativity, risk-taking, presentation and performance. And let this expressive part of being human be the heart through which children come to beauty, collaboration, literature and agency, and unfold.

Let an understanding of design and systems thinking be built into this from an early age. We can learn about feedback and complexity through role-plays and reflecting on experience. Designing and making things – whether it be systems or objects – is fundamental to developing a sense of agency; let designing and making be seen as a high achievement of humanity alongside the arts, knowledge of the past, maths and science.

Let philosophy, or epistemology to be precise, be another constituent dimension of learning. What do we know? How do we know it? What does it mean to know something? What is reliable evidence? This area would include much that is currently done under the titles of science, history and geography but without any fragmentation into subjects. As children become interested in describing and understanding the world they will need maths to make sense of it. But let not maths be considered superior to storytelling, for example. Let compulsory subjects and disciplines disappear.

Let the development of all these things, together with functional numeracy and literacy, curiosity, collaboration, communication and empathy, be the aims against which education is valued. Educational initiatives funded from public money need to be accountable. Let the evaluation regimes be participatory with all stakeholders involved in a constant cycle of action and reflection, of setting goals and trying things out and then seeing in what ways they move things forward. These goals will vary from place to place and indeed be rooted in local aspirations and needs. In this way the initiatives will be seen as a part of a complex system and their development be feedback-driven.

Appendix C

Once a week Olly, a sixteen-year-old, meets with mentor Alex to review progress and plan activity over the next seven days. This might take place in the café or some pleasant open space, or in a special meeting room. Olly is getting increasingly interested in coding and Alex recommends a new course that will run for three hours a day over six weeks. Olly contacts the course leader and discusses joining the group but is advised to follow a Khan Academy introduction to coding[94] before applying. The course leader also advises Olly to find a real project. Olly makes an appointment with a resources manager to see if there is a local business or community group who can provide a project brief to run alongside the course. It turns out there is a local environmental community group that needs to redesign its website, and Olly arranges to meet them one evening but that won't be for a month. Olly is apprehensive about meeting the community group, so Alex advises attending a drop-in communication skills workshop that is being run by some actors. This will help Olly build the confidence to meet with the community group.

One evening a week Olly trains with a football team and helps the under-8s as an assistant to the team coach. Often this takes Olly to a match on a Saturday. Olly has been asked by the football club to organise a five-a-side tournament in the summer. This means phone calls to other clubs, fixing a venue and finding referees, but Olly is unsure whether to take this on.

Olly belongs to a band and once a week they use a studio in the learning exchange for practice. They also need to raise money for a decent amp for gigs, so through the learning exchange they find some temporary paid work. Before they do this they attend a workshop on safety and how to deal with possible threatening work situations. This includes role-play on dealing with sexual harassment and shouting, abusive behaviour.

Olly has a long-term interest in music technology and realises that, in any engineering activity, maths and physics need to be up to speed. Olly belongs to a physics class that runs every day based on a flipped learning model. The tutor gives the group an assignment and they have to find the information they need on the web; the classes are for peer-to-peer learning and dealing with any problems that emerge. Often these can be resolved within the group and the tutor just chairs the discussions, though occasionally an expert input is required. Some of the group are planning to sit an Institute of Physics exam at some time in the future, but this is not a priority, more an add-on. The maths is done at the moment through Khan Academy courses and at lunchtimes there is an open session with a maths tutor for individuals to ask questions. Some of Olly's friends are also doing maths and they can help each other. Meanwhile, Olly is using the maker lab to renovate an old bass amp that was being thrown out by an uncle. This is getting him interested in analogue electronics.

Olly also works in the community café for three hours a week, which provides a small but regular income. Alex is impressed by Olly's range of activities (and so is Olly!) but wonders if there might be more in the area of creative arts. Making a video is one possibility, maybe linked to the band? Or joining a writing group to develop original lyrics? These ideas are on hold at the moment as Olly is so busy, but Alex has asked the resources team at the learning exchange if there might be others interested in a creative writing group that could focus on song-writing.

In all these activities Olly and fellow students are taking responsibility for their learning but under the guidance of Alex and other mentors. Often the groups will include people of all ages, especially the possible creative writing group.

One of Alex's roles is to make sure that Olly keeps a diary and at the end of any activity or project does a review and evaluation. This will include some record that may be on paper but more likely to be a digital record. In this way Olly builds up a portfolio of activities over the years. It may well be useful if Olly applies for a job in the future, demonstrating a wide range of skills and achievements. It will also be useful if Olly applies for a formal university or college course. But its main value lies in encouraging Olly to be a reflective and responsible learner.

Hopefully Ollie will also find some time to chill with mates!

REFERENCES

All internet links last accessed on 15th April 2021

PART I

[1] https://www.cam.ac.uk/news/socrates-was-guilty-as-charged

[2] Waterfield, R. (2009). *Why Socrates Died: Dispelling the Myths.* London: Faber and Faber.

[3] Rowe, J. (2001). Socrates. In: J. Palmer, ed., *Fifty Major Thinkers in Education; From Confucius to Dewey.* Milton Park: Routledge.

[4] Hobson, P. (2001). Aristotle. In: J. Palmer, ed., *op.cit.*

[5] https://en.wikipedia.org/wiki/Philosophy_of_education#Avicenna

[6] Steitieh, D. M. (2001). In: Ibn Tufayl. In J. Palmer, ed. *op cit.*

[7] This is drawn largely from https://fr.wikipedia.org/wiki/École_mutuelle

[8] Cohen, A. (1981). The Educational Philosophy of Tolstoy. *Oxford Review of Education,* 7 (3) pp241-251.

[9] Crosby, E.H. (1904). *Tolstoy as a schoolmaster.* Chicago, The Hammersmark Publishing Co.

[10] Dewey, J. (1907). "The School and Social Progress." Chapter 1 in *The School and Society*. Chicago: The University of Chicago Press. Retrieved 11/09/15 from https://www.brocku.ca/MeadProject/Dewey/Dewey_1907/Dewey_1907a.html

[11] Apple, M.W. and Teitelbaum, K. (2001) John Dewey 1859-1952. In: J. Palmer, ed., *op cit* p180.

[12] Apple, M.W. and Teitelbaum, K. (2001). In: J. Palmer, ed., *op. cit.* p 181.

[13] Pitt, J and Pavlova, M (2001). Pedagogy in Transition: from Labour Training to Humanistic Technology Education in Russia. In S. Webber and I. Liikaned, eds., *Education and Civic Culture in Post-Communist Societies*. Basingstoke: Palgrave.

[14] When published in 1970 there was not the same awareness of language and gender as there is today.

[15] Freire, P. (1970). *Pedagogy of the Oppressed*. (English edition). Harmondsworth: Penguin, p 46.

[16] Freire, P. (1970). *op cit* p50.

[17] Illich, I. (1973). *Deschooling society*. Harmondsworth: Penguin, p11.

[18] Illich, I. (1973). *op cit* p9.

[19] Ken Robinson described the difference between education and training through this anecdote. "If my daughter comes back from school and says she has sex education lessons, I think that's fine. If she comes back from school saying she has had sex training .... Well, that's quite different!"

[20] https://en.wikipedia.org/wiki/Waldorf_education

[21] See Hirsch's Core Knowledge Foundation on www.coreknowledge.org

[22] www.theguardian.com/education/2018/apr/10/lesson-battle-why-teachers-lining-up-leave

[23] www.theguardian.com/education/2018/may/13/teacher-burnout-shortages-recruitment-problems-budget-cuts

[24] www.independent.co.uk/voices/teachers-crisis-education-leaving-profession-jobs-market-droves-who-would-be-one-a7591821.html

[25] https://www.theguardian.com/commentisfree/2018/aug/31/teacher-shortage-maths-science-pay-rise-government

[26] www.theguardian.com/education/2018/oct/04/teacher-crisis-hits-london-as-nearly-half-quit-within-five-years

[27] https://www.tes.com/news/recruitment-third-teachers-leaving-profession-within-5-years

[28] See for example Pitsoe, V. and Letseka, M. (2013). Foucault's Discourse and Power: Implications for Instructionist Classroom Management. *Open Journal of Philosophy, 3*(1), pp23-28.

[29] Gatto, J. T. (1992). *Dumbing Us Down - The Hidden Curriculum of Compulsory Schooling.* (Anniversary edition) Gabriola Island BC: New Society Publishers

[30] https://www.unicef.org.uk/wp-content/uploads/2010/05/UNCRC_summary-1.pdf

[31] Burke, B. (1999, 2005). Antonio Gramsci, schooling and education. In *The Encyclopaedia of Pedagogy and Informal Education*. Found on http://www.infed.org/thinkers/et-gram.htm.

[32] Caplan, B. (2018). *The Case against Education: Why the Education System Is a Waste of Time and Money*. Princeton; Oxford: Princeton University Press.

PART 2

[33] Zohar II, 184a; Sperling and Simon, *The Zohar*, Vol. IV, p. 125.

[34] http://www.unfpa.org/migration

[35] http://www.dailymail.co.uk/news/article-4003756/Robots-steal-15m-jobs-says-bank-chief-Doom-laden-Carney-warns-middle-classes-hollowed-new-technology.html

[36] http://archive.spectator.co.uk/article/2nd-september-1960/25/subsidising-films

[37] https://www.theguardian.com/uk/2005/sep/27/labourconference.speeches

[38] Sally Hunt (General Secretary of the University and College Union) as reported in https://www.theguardian.com/uk-news/2016/nov/16/universities-accused-of-importing-sports-direct-model-for-lecturers-pay

[39] http://www.bbc.co.uk/news/uk-22007058

[40] https://en.wikipedia.org/wiki/Rentier_capitalism

[41] See for example https://www.politico.eu/article/isds-the-most-toxic-acronym-in-europe/

[42] For a fuller description of corporate welfare see http://www.corporate-welfare-watch.org.uk/wp/corporate-welfare/

43 https://www.tax.org.uk/media-centre/blog/media-and-politics/review-rsa-debate-business-tax-reliefs-corporate-welfare-or

44 https://www.theguardian.com/environment/damian-carrington-blog/2015/oct/22/hinkley-point-uk-energy-policy-is-now-hunkering-in-a-nuclear-bunker

45 https://www.equalitytrust.org.uk/taken-ride-how-uk-public-transport-subsidies-entrench-inequality

46 https://www.tribunemag.co.uk/2020/05/corporate-welfare-is-not-the-exception-its-the-rule

47 Lonergan, E. and Blyth, M. (2020). *Angrynomics*. Newcastle upon Tyne: Agenda Publishing.

48 https://www.imf.org/external/pubs/ft/fandd/2019/09/tackling-global-tax-havens-shaxon.htm

49 https://delong.typepad.com/kalecki43.pdf

50 See for example https://neweconomics.org/2018/10/a-government-is-not-a-household

51 A review of Guilluy, C. (2019). *Twilight of the Elites* can be found on https://www.theguardian.com/books/2019/jan/17/twilight-of-the-elites-christophe-guilluy-review

52 Goodhart, D. (2017). *The Road to Somewhere: The Populist Revolt and the Future of Politics*. London: Hurst Publishers

53 http://www.cbi.org.uk/news/education-is-more-than-knowledge-alone/

54 https://www.tes.com/news/school-news/breaking-views/long-last-narrow-knowledge-based-curriculum-being-rejected-across

55 Carson, K. (2018). Libertarian Municipalism: Networked Cities as Resilient Platforms for Post-Capitalist Transition https://www.researchgate.net/publication/323542606_Libertarian_Municipalism_Networked_Cities_as_Resilient_Platforms_for_Post-Capitalist_Transition

56 https://ecovillage.org/projects/

57 https://www.synathina.gr/en/synathina/about-us.html

58 https://www.youtube.com/watch?v=5KQOckZzxAY

59 https://ajuntament.barcelona.cat/digital/en

60 https://ajuntament.barcelona.cat/digital/en/digital-innovation/make-in-bcn/poblenou-maker-district

61 https://www.weareeveryone.org

[62] https://tessybritton.medium.com/universal-basic-everything-f149afc4cef1

[63] Pitt, J. & Keane, M. (1984). *Community Organising? You've never really tried it! The challenge to Britain from the USA*. London: London Voluntary Service Council

[64] See https://www.citizensuk.org/about-us/who-we-are/

[65] See https://locality.org.uk

[66] Carson, K. (2018). *op. cit.*

[67] Monbiot, G. (2017). *Out of the Wreckage: A new Politics for an Age of Crisis*. London and New York: Verso, pp 97/8.

[68] Monbiot, G. (2017) *op. cit.* p 100.

[69] https://www.nytimes.com/2020/12/29/business/cooperatives-basque-spain-economy.html

[70] https://www.preston.gov.uk/article/1339/What-is-Preston-Model-

[71] https://www.preston.gov.uk/media/1792/How-we-built-community-wealth-in-Preston/pdf/CLES_Preston_Document_WEB_AW.pdf?m=636994067328930000

[72] Lindenfeld, F. and Wynn, P. (2012). *Why Do Some Worker Co-ops Succeed While Others Fail? The Role of Internal and External Social Factors.* Grassroots Economic Organizing (GEO) https://geo.coop/story/why-some-worker-co-ops-succeed-while-others-fail

[73] Ibid

[74] https://coinstreet.org

[75] See, for example, https://geo.coop , https://locality.org.uk , https://www.uk.coop

[76] Taken from *The history of basic income* which is based on Van Parijs, P. & Vanderborght, Y. (2017) *Basic Income. A Radical Proposal for a Free Society and a Sane Economy.* Cambridge MA: Harvard University Press *accessed* on http://basicincome.org/basic-income/history/

[77] http://basicincome.org/

[78] Lonergan, E. and Blyth, M. (2020). *Angrynomics.* Newcastle upon Tyne: Agenda Publishing.

[79] https://citizensclimatelobby.uk/climate-income/policy-makers/carbon-fee-dividend/

[80] https://www.jrf.org.uk/report/where-next-universal-credit-and-tackling-poverty

[81] https://www.citymetric.com/politics/granting-planning-permission-massively-increases-land-values-shouldnt-state-get-share-1154

[82] http://basicincome.org/

[83] See https://www.youtube.com/watch?v=6IBE-oWSiTHc

[84] https://www.theguardian.com/world/2020/aug/18/female-led-countries-handled-coronavirus-better-study-jacinda-ardern-angela-merkel

[85] https://www.ft.com/content/6b597385-ba51-413a-96bd-cb75d3446718

[86] https://www.circularconversations.com/conversations/follow-energy-patterns-to-build-healthy-systems

[87] See https://connected-communities.org/

Part 3

[88] https://www.khanacademy.org/

[89] See www.thoughtco.com/all-about-platos-famous-academy-112520

[90] http://www.edutopia.org/project-based-learning-history

[91] https://en.wikipedia.org/wiki/Project-based_learning

[92] https://www.theguardian.com/politics/2018/apr/02/pay-all-uk-25-year-olds-a-10000-inheritance-says-thinktank

[93] The term 'meta-learning' was originally described by Donald B. Maudsley (1979). (See http://en.wikipedia.org/wiki/Meta_learning)

[94] https://www.khanacademy.org/computing/hour-of-code/hour-of-code-tutorial/v/welcome-hour-of-code

THE AUTHORS

JAMES PITT FRSA

Apart from a few years as a joiner, James has spent most of his working life in and around education. Many years were in informal education where he was a neighbourhood organiser. He has taught in schools and universities and was senior research fellow in the education department at the University of York. He has been deeply engaged in curriculum development and teacher training, especially in England and Russia. James' specialist areas are design, and education for a circular economy. Author of some 40 plus articles and books on education, he has been pondering what it all adds up to. With five children of his own, not to mention grandchildren and a great-granddaughter, the future of education is close to his heart. This book is born of reflecting on that experience.

KEN WEBSTER

Most of Ken's working life has been in education, either formally as a secondary school teacher, a lecturer in higher education or as an educational consultant developing educational resources and programmes internationally. He was significant in the development of contemporary ideas around the circular economy and was Head of Innovation for the Ellen MacArthur Foundation (2010-2018). Ken is currently a Visiting Fellow at Cranfield University and a member of the Club of Rome's 21st Century Transformational Economics Commission. He is author of a number of books including Circular Economy: A Wealth of Flows (2017), The Wonderful Circles of Oz (A Circular Economy Story) with Alex Duff (2021) and Sense and Sustainability (2009) with Craig Johnson. Ken holds that education and critical thinking are central to all constructive change.